SING UP!

First published in 2008 by
The Dedalus Press
13 Moyclare Road
Baldoyle
Dublin 13
Ireland

www.dedaluspress.com

ISBN 978 1 904556 97 8

Dedalus Press titles are represented in North America
by Syracuse University Press, Inc., 621 Skytop Road,
Suite 110, Syracuse, New York 13244, and in the UK by
Central Books, 99 Wallis Road, London E9 5LN

Printed in Ireland by Johnswood Press, Dublin

Typesetting & design: Pat Boran
Cover image © Ferran Traite Soler

The Dedalus Press receives financial assistance from
An Chomhairle Ealaíon / The Arts Council, Ireland

SING UP!

Irish Comic Songs & Satires
for Every Occasion

collected and introduced by
Fintan Vallely

And including songs by

Finbar Boyle, Hugh Collins, Patsy Cronin, George Curtin,
Crawford Howard, Dónal Lehane, Tim Lyons, Jim McAllister,
Mickey McConnell, Fred McCormick, Brian McGuinness,
Adam McNaughton, John Maguire, Mícheál Marrinan,
Sheila Miller, Andy Mitchell, Sean Mone, Joe Mulheron,
Ciarán Ó Drisceoil, Con Ó Drisceoil, Brian O'Rourke,
Déaglán Tallon, Fintan Vallely and Bill Watkins.

DEDALUS PRESS
DUBLIN, IRELAND

Thanks, to

Julian Vignoles and Joe Mulheron who gave vital breaks to this all; to Christy Moore for having the guts to sing some of it; to Tim Lyons for the crack and companionship on tour, Tommy Munnelly for the silent signposting, Frank Becchofer for the years of gigs; Peta Webb, Ken Hall, Arthur Johnston and John Waltham for the organisation; Anna Lyons, Francie Brolly, Constance Short, Nicholas Carolan, Caoilte Breatnach, Harry Bradshaw, Éamonn Ó Bróithe and Joe Corcoran for words and information; to Eoghanie Ó Súilleabháin for DNA screening of songwriter resources in West Cork; to Bríd McSweeney and Danny Maidhicí Ó Súilleabháin for accounts of movements; to all the songwriters for co-operation and permission—particularly Tim Lyons, Mícheál Marrinan and Crawford Howard for generous consideration, to Gerry O'Hanlon, Patricia Flynn, Jimmy McBride, An Góilín, Liam Morrissey, Nenagh Singers and Jim Walsh for providing the venues; to the local governments for the power and the glory that produced such icons to assail; to the clergy of Ireland for policing regulation so tenaciously and yet being so outrageously, colourfully human as to be simultaneously guilty of all the sins for which they have been roasting their flocks for centuries; to all the MEPs without whose moral transgressions we'd know nothing and have no awareness of anything liberal beyond the dunghill; to Pádraig Flynn who so patiently educated us about women; to all our presidents and candidates, the athletes, soccer and rugby players, the Olympic swimmers, runners and boxers who manufacture and challenge assaults on Irish identity; to *The Irish Independent* for inspiring incendiary outrage and articulate analysis among the citizenry; to Guinness Ireland on account of whom we are obliged to associate music with an arrogant logo perpetually shoved in our faces. Long live *Beamish* and poteen, *The Frying Irishman, Chuck Wagon, Miss Ellie's, Rice Paddy* and the non-Imperialist huckster and mobile troughsters who water and fodder the good crack. Thanks too to the non-official, productive environment, the voluntarily-run labyrinths of Irish life wherein alone it is possible for all this muddle of observation, unqualified and unmediated opinion, singing of all kinds, to survive.

Above all, most sincere thanks to Evelyn Conlon, Warren and Trevor, for putting up with the insanity.

—FV

Documentary information on all of the songs in this book may be found at **www.singup.eu**.

Contents

Preface

This gather-up of intolerance, irreverence, slagging and sedition was inspired by myself and Tim Lyon's performing as *Schitheredee* in the years after 1987. In that duet we experimented on the natives of Scotland with satires, send-ups and other ephemera. These we had constructed out of frustration with the gap in the 'Traditional' style of Irish ballad making which had left singers devoid of any up to date comic material other than Val Doonican songs. The idea was to rush out a book of our own songs in 1988, but somehow it never got finished. However, having had plenty of time since to talk about it to others, and with singing and playing all over the place in the meantime, the idea expanded, and it seemed only right to give others a fair crack of the whip. Once started on this course, other souls parched in the woodwork, who had been doing the same thing for years, became obvious, and here there are seventy six songs representing the work of twenty-four writers.

Most of the events commemorated in the lyrics took place over the 1980s and1990s. The songs document the huge changes in Irish culture and society inside a small number of years. These transformations were brought about by the invention of the aeroplane (the Pope), British colonisation of Malaya (rubber), the Famine (a desire to stuff the country with chips), the television (politics), the chopping down of the rain forests (the weather, depression and artificial pubs), EC grain mountains (too much beer), Siúcra Éireann (poteen), third level education (too much analysis) and the use of telecommunications in religious fundamentalism (rampant idolatry). The territory is mostly modern Ireland in all its miseries, elations and protest, change and no change; its fulfilments, compromises, oppressions, slavish copycatting, inferiority complexes and under-development—cultural everything-cum-nothing. The songs' themes therefore underlie culture today and the verses are in the mould of both the 19th century seditious ballad and the music-hall skit. Moral judgement masquerades as wit in the best tradition of lightening the load. The tunes are mostly standard old song airs, hard-working music shop-dummies that have been dressed and re-dressed in response to fashions with scores of different sets of words over the centuries[1].

No notation is given, for these songs are most effectively sung in the 'Traditional' style—to a variety of metrically-suitable airs, unaccompanied, bendable and potentially response-generating.

COMPOSITION AND GENDER

Many of the songwriters featured here have long ago given up composition. This is because, through any one topic, observations and expressions which would also be applied to other subjects are 'used up'. Thus the comic/satirical versifier usually arrives at a blank wall much more quickly than other kinds of writer, and so, though fulfilled and content, retirement comes early for them. There is too in this book the, ahem, rather glaring absence of women writers. Several of the pieces are sourced from women indeed, but alas, only one is from a XX chromosome nib. This is no oversight, for there are many women writing songs in the Traditional music scene. But the tendency has been, on the singing circuits of the 1990s, for them to be less concerned on the humour front, and more with getting serious things said (or maybe the Y-front of the species uses humour to avoid thinking too deeply?).

CONSEQUENCES AND HAZARDS

The songs are very much of their era, and what is funny today may not be so tomorrow when the subject of the song is history. But the greater danger with satirical verse is that it might be—heaven forbid—perhaps taken personally or seen as offensive. For instance, in the middle of verse three of 'The Johnnies Song' being sung in a certain town in south Donegal back in '89, the singer was set upon by a transmogrified National School headmaster at three in the morning on a Sunday night. As the complainant was dragged away roaring incoherently about 'The Faith!', he enunciated the eloquent epithet: "If you ever show your fuckin' face around Mountc- again I'll knock your fuckin' teeth down your fuckin' throat." Perhaps he was showing off his remarkable attentive powers for one so far gone—in that he remembered 'The Ballad of the Teeth'. But he apologised publicly for it all later—after the effects of the song had worn off. Also, in July 1995, in far-off Spilimbergo, up in northern Italy close to the Slovenian border, the singing of 'The Moving Statues' unleashed a similar reaction from a young Irish cleric who interpreted the sentiment as 'Unionist'. Back in Derry, in Ireland itself, the same politico-religious reaction necessitated the exit of the singer of 'The Statues' through the back window of a nationalist bar.

This serves to underline that not everyone is impressed by satirical political/current affairs song. But then not everyone reads car magazines or watches *The X Factor*, the *Eurovision* song contest or *Big Brother*. Sometimes people object out of a sense of outrage that politics can be allowed make its way into leisure at all. But more often—as with comedian Hal Roach[2]—it is specifically the singer's actual or implied point of view that is objected to. The problem is not new, being recorded in print in 1885 at the height of Music-hall's comic and sentimental song popularity. Then, *The Era,* the paper for the English licensed vintner's trade, railed:

> ...it is one of the greatest nuisances possible to sensible people who go to places of amusement to divert their minds from politics and business alike to have the opinions of the daily papers reproduced in verse and flung at their heads by a music hall singer. Persons who go to a place of amusement to be amused, and these, we believe, form the steadily paying class, are too sensible to care to proclaim their private opinions by applauding mindless rubbish with a political meaning.[3]

All ballads and folksongs are the original works of anthropology, sociology and politics in the lives of country people and the migrant poor of the towns. They chart the lives of the 'Folk'—the people whose existences were the worse for not having *Burke's Landed Gentry* [4] detail their male seed, breed and generation. This particular collection is of the social/political kind—the type of thing which might be seen on the news, but interpreted by the writers satirically or cynically out of an abhorrence of sentimentality. Points are made, horses—dead and otherwise—flogged, and survival springs from the debris. Anyway, the overall slant has already been accounted for in the mid-18th century words of Dr. Johnson: "The Irish are a fair people. They never speak well of one another."

Part 1: Diddley Dee

WILLIE MAC BRIDE: THE REVENGE

Some time in the 1970s, Australian Eric Bogle wrote a wonderful (so to speak) song about the horrors of World War 1. It dealt with the pointlessness of the slaughter, and addressed an unknown soldier, one Willie MacBride. *The Fureys* recorded it and it became a hit, reaching the top of the charts and staying lodged in everybody's sentiment file, everywhere that English is spoken. Overnight it replaced Thomas Moore's *Believe me if all these endearing young charms, Goodnight Irene* and *Paper Roses* as the No. 1 wedding-guest song. From that oxygen-rare pedestal of success it veered downward into the average shower-routine repertoire, and finally it arrived in the weekend-night, lounge-bar circuit—in which emotional surroundings it could be dealt full, deliberate, slow and painful lyric justice. By the early eighties it was already having the effect of mustard gas in the pubs and there were rumours of a *fatwah* being put out on Eric Bogle for writing it. Anyone who was suspected of being able to sing was constantly terrorised by unknown civilians with requests to "do Willie MacBride". Finally Crawford Howard from Belfast—a renowned composer of satires— went insane and decided he would oblige—with parody, as revenge.

***

Willie Mac Bride: The Revenge

Have you heard of the song about Willie Mac Bride?
If I hear it again it'll turn me inside.
For it's sung in the Springtime, it's sung in the Fall,
And mostly by people who can't sing at all.
You go down to the bar on a Saturday night
For a pint and a song, and things are all right
'Till some drunken punter slumps down by your side,—saying:
"Sing us that song about Willie Mac Bride."
Now you say you don't know it—but this will not do,
For now he's determined to sing it to you,
And he spills half your drink and starts off in a key
That was never invented on land or on sea!
And as things go on sure the whole thing gets worse
For you now realise that he knows every verse.
With his arm round your shoulder—for now he's your friend—
He's going to sing the damn thing to the end.

CHORUS:
Did they sing the song badly?
Did they drink the pints gladly?
Did the drunks fall asleep as they lowered them down?
Did the barman cry "Last Drinks!" in chorus
Did the punters cry "Thank Christ that's over!"

You go out to the 'Gents' for a quarter of an hour
And you watch the TV in the old Public Bar,
And then you come back thinking that he will tire
But he's still going on about gas and barbed wire.
And ten minutes later you're now in a trance
For he's up to his oxters in the Green Fields of France,
The punters are quiet—you won't hear a peep—
And you now realise that they've all gone to sleep.
CHORUS

Oh, Willie Mac Bride why the hell did you die?
The trouble you'd have saved if you'd come back alive.
If you'd got a good job, or signed on the b'roo—
We'd not have to listen to songs about you.
But still I don't know now—I'm glad that you're dead
With the green Fields of France piled up over your head;
For the trouble you've caused since the day that you died
Oh, shootin's too good for you, Willie Mac Bride.
CHORUS

Now listen, Mac Bride, what the hell is your game
With a photograph stuck in a mouldy old frame?
You can buy them in Smithfield at 10p a throw,
So what's all the fuss about I'd like to know?
And what's all this talk about barbed wire and smoke?
Sure you shouldn't have joined if you can't take a joke!
We don't give a damn where the red poppies dance,
Oh, Willie Mac Bride, will you give us a chance!
CHORUS

(Schitheredee version appears in Appendix 2, page 240.
The song can be heard sung by everybody.)

'Standards' are a beast which terrorise the body music throughout the length and breadth of Ireland. These have been effectively moulded by various Radio Éireann and RTÉ personnel over the years by selecting and choosing what the public eventually get to hear. But, faced with the pressing need to establish supremacy based on competitive talent in music and song (as opposed to 'success' in the commercial world) the powers that be in the structured life of Traditional music—Comhaltas Ceoltóirí Éireann—have had to adopt the concept of adjudicator, arguably a necessary evil in a competitive world. At a certain All-Ireland Fleadh Cheoil in a certain place in a certain year, a certain adjudicator took a set *agin* the Ulster folk and had a go at Comber man Jackie Boyce's style of singing as not being *kosher*[5]. The heckles were riz, the 'Ulster style' took to the barricades and the adjudicator was roasted upon the spit of satire, upon which device he is occasionally turned at singing weekends—just to make sure no-one forgets that indeed everybody does have standards. The air is *'The Bogs of Shanaheever',* originally a sentimental song about a greyhound.

***

The Free State Adjudicator

(Air: 'The Bogs of Shanaheever')

At these oul' gatherins for years, well it always made me weary
For to hear those oul' boys sing their big ballads long and dreary.
But my mother said: "Son, sing!" and nothin' would placate her,
So it was down to the Fleadh, and the fleadh cheoil adjudicator.

I practised hard for days, songs of love and of Napoleon,
Learned not to sing 'till I was asked three times—the false starts and the
    loud coughin'.
I would catch the *fear a' tí's* eye to stop that oul' diddley-dee—none braver
Then it's down to Listowel, and the fleadh cheoil adjudicator.

With me gold earring and cowboy boots, me bomber jacket I was wearin',
"It's a bloody Fleadh Cowboy!" I heard yer man a'swearin',
When I rolled a wee cheroot, put it behind me ear for later,
"Well! By god—he's on the drugs!" says the Free State adjudicator.

In Fermanagh now for years they've been plagued by Paddy Tunney
And Brian Murphy in Forkhill would only sing for the big money,
But there's none of them I feared, none of them I favoured,
Until I was betrayed by a Free State adjudicator.

He said the Ulster Style was wrong and my choice of song was shockin',
And my ornamentation nil, boys, I was goin' to clock him.
My song had been sung by the Fenian Men, the bard John Reilly later.
"You got that from Christy Moore," says this Free State adjudicator.

My Parish Priest sang next, and I saw me chances fadin',
The adjudicator smiled, green-and-brown scapulars round him trailin'.
When I dropped my carry-out—the bottle of Buckfast I did break her!
The Pioneer pin began to glow on the lapel of the adjudicator.

Up to Dublin he'd been sent for two days intensive trainin',
Buyin' MacMathúna pints, his certificate a'gainin'.
He thought 'Seán Nós' was the boy who might join the session later,
And from Monkstown he emerged, an expert adjudicator.

When Ireland is set free by young men and women brave and darin',
And Belfast will host at last a Fleadh Cheoil na hÉireann,
All informers will be shot, every rogue and every traitor,
And a last song we'll request from all Free State Adjudicators.

© *Joseph Mulheron*

*'The Bogs of Shanaheever', the original melody of this song can be heard on
Sean Garvey's album* Out of the Ground *(1998) www.seangarvey.ie*

For many, many years, one-time accordionist Eamon McGivney dragged his chains around the townlands of County Clare as an Ordnance Survey man, heir to the heroes of Brien Friel's play *Translations* which tells how our placenames got their anglicised descriptive abominations. Originally he played the accordion, but having coming to live in Clare, on TV one day he witnessed Tony MacMahon anguishing over proper-sounding instruments, so he discreetly slipped away and parked his Lamborghini forever and bought himself a fiddle. Now he's fully competent at authenticity and can hold his head up anywhere, especially on RTÉ. Dame Fortune, however, got her own back and visited modernism on him again. Now his job, which used to involve walking for miles, pencils, theodolites, paper, drawing boards and public houses in quaint places, is all surveyed by camera from an airplane and drawn up on a computer screen. On his behalf, Déaglán Tallon composed this epitaph to his great service to the nation. The air is 'The Plains of Drishane' (not the Ordnance Survey planes).

***

The Ordnance Survey Man

(Air: 'The Plains of Drishane')

My trade and occupation and professional vocation
Concerns the use of level, theodolite and chain.
My notes on elevation done with much perambulation
Will aid your navigation on side-car or on train;
And at expert mensuration or precise triangulation
I am noted for my patience and my steadiness of hand,
Calculations topographic, observations demographic
And exertions cartographic; I'm the Ordnance Survey Man.

When I was but of tender years my mother shed great lakes of tears
As I struck out bereft of fears and headed for The Park.[6]
But with my melodious disposition and my angelic composition
I was bound for perdition with my fiddle on my back.
Thus the tunes extemporaneous I would render quite spontaneous,
And my work became extraneous as I wandered o'er the land,
And at cross-roads quite congruent the people were influenced
By the music mellifluent of the Ordnance Survey Man.

And as time passed by I gained in fame, 'twasn't long before I made my name,
And I joined in the game to plot the surface of the moon.
The lunar landscape I perceived, notoriety I soon achieved
For circumnavigating it by boat and by balloon.
And the Sea of Tranquillity, extending to infinity,
I expounded on most wittily and on the fish that swim therein.
So on account of my ability and my extraordinary virility
The world became acquainted with the Ordnance Survey Man.

From there 'twas but a step so terse to encompass all the Universe
And to scribble the co-ordinates of Jupiter and Mars.
Through the Galaxy unfailingly I journeyed uncomplainingly
And worked quite entertainingly adjacent to the stars.
And the angels non-terrestrial and choristers celestial
Would cease their labours vestial as I passed them on my way
They would flap their wings and shout such things like,
"Yerra Eamonn, how's she cuttin' boy?"
For they were so much taken by the Ordnance Survey Man.

But of all my great accomplishments, narrated less embellishments,
Related with veracity and recounted with *élan,*
Was a scheme so diabolical, with undertones quite comical,
And nuances anatomical, it was a mighty plan;
For to chart all licenced premises and to publish their blemishes,
Every tavern with false blandishments, every pub without a slate,
And purveyors of bad pints, also conveyors of Ringosporeum
Where surveyors get dingdoreum, says the Ordinance Survey Man.

So let me state it without vanity: I laboured for humanity
And nearly lost my sanity, my life's work to complete.
For it was my great ambition to launch the first edition
Of *McGivney's Topers' Almanac and Guide to Drinking Beer.*
And on entering pubs most gallantly or being thrown out with profanity
By hunchbacked cranky barsmen or peddlers of bad wine,
I braved all molestation and suffered deprivation
To gain this information, says the Ordnance Survey Man.

And compiling this compendium, all its chapters and addendium,
I collated it with pride and annotated it with care;
Containing data so meticulous on publicans ridiculous
And especially those who'd sicken us, oh this manuscript is rare.
So convey this great canonical on your journeys alcoholical,
Expeditions gastronomical and embarrassment 'twill save,
For 'tis worth all of the world to know which is fair and which is horrible,
This document's infallible, says the Ordnance Survey Man.

So maintain your contemplation and your mighty meditation
No matter what your station, be it work or be it play;
Bear in mind my efforts strenuous and my penmanship so generous
To guide your feet through tenuous without leading you astray.
And in company nefarious, lively or gregarious
Or otherwise contrarious, hilarious or bland,
With this map in hand you're armed so grand and life you'll face courageous
And avoid disease contagious with the Ordnance Survey Man.

Ah! But now in my advancing age 'tis time I shuffled off the stage
To leave behind the world's rage for Mullagh by the sea,
And on evenings much imbibable with my colleagues so convivial
We'll gather there at Ollie's for a pint or maybe three.
And 'tis there I'll live contentedly, surrounded most enchantingly
By my sons thirteen and daughters three, all warriors of our race,
And I will wander home without disgrace to linger in the sweet embrace
Of the dark-haired girl from Clare who loves the Ordnance Survey Man.

© *Déaglán Tallon*

Tune names are held in great reverence by some, and for these a tune is umbilically attached to its title. Others know no names at all, and simply play the music as learnt. Sometimes the tune takes on the name of the person who made it, or the player who first recorded it, or from whom it was first heard. There is additionally a range of tune names which is as informative as a decade by decade inventory of technical and social progress from the year 1750 or so onwards. There is occasional double meaning and sexual innuendo, but overall the titles are reference points for a place, event, animal, feeling, object of desire or person. Thus we have 'The Strawberry Beds', 'Turkeys in the Straw', 'The Mountain Lark', 'Farewell to Erin', 'Miss Thornton's', 'The Gudgeon of Morris's Car', 'Tady's Wattle', 'Roll Her in the Ryegrass', 'Hartigan's Fancy', 'Sailing into Walpole's Marsh' and so on. It can be confusing when a tune has more than one title—the result of bad memory, inventive pragmatism and/or someone seeking to gain radio-play royalties for a tune they didn't compose. Whatever the cause, for those with trouble remembering their repertoire, accordionist Michael Scanlan has for several years advocated a final solution of memorising it all as a scripted air. This piece takes him to heart by referencing over 100 tunes, about one third of the average player's tally.

***

Last Night's Fun

(Air: 'Phil the Fluter's Ball')

The Muses nine with me combined to aid me with their lyres.
They worked with me while in a dream, to chart my repertoire.
Highlands, polkas, jigs, reels, marches, airs, hornpipes and slides,
Titles set to Phil the Fluter's fantasy as guide.
Last night in session in *The Tap Room* with *The Lads of Laois*
The Whinny Hills of Leitrim rang to *Bonaparte's Retreat;*
I'd drifted off in slumber to the crooning of *The Dairymaid*
And came to in *The Sally Gardens* close to *Peter Street.*

Sporting Mollie, Tim Moloney and *The Mistress of the House*
On *The Rocky Road to Dublin* over by *The Templehouse,*
Mamma's Pet, Colonel Fraser and *The Boys of Ballisodare*
Rode with *The Yellow Tinker* on his *Jockey to the Fair,*

Then *Faral Gara* shouts: "We're off to hear *The Kilfenora*"—"I
Don't Care, says *Roarin' Mary*, "I just want *One Bottle More.*"
"Well, we've *Money in both Pockets*," cried *The Bucks of Oranmore*,
"So come and *Toss the Feathers* with us on *The Cliffs of Moher.*"

Well I met *The Star of Munster* too, she roared "Go *Ride a Mile!*"
To *The Hag with the Money* who'd come from *The Plains of Boyle.*
The Carrowcastle Lasses—Up Against the Boughalauns—
Sent *The Galway Rambler* for *The Ravelled Hank of Yarn.*
"*Follow Me Up to Carlow!*" says *Lady Ann Montgomery,*
"To *The Congress at the Cornerhouse* that's run by *Captain Rock.*
Old Man Dillon's speaking on the *Jacksons* in *The Upper Room*
And *Corney is Coming* with *Kregg's Pipes* to play *The Beauty Spot.*"

I joined *The Dunmore Lasses* as they sang *The Sligo Chorus*
To the music of *The Skylark* over in *The Laurel Groves.*
There we met *The Duke of Leinster* with *Lord Gordon* on *The Sunny Banks*
Discussing with *The Dusty Miller—How the Money Goes.*
In came *Lord McDonald* with the woman known as *Miss McLeod*
But *Early in the Morning, On the Sly* he said to me:
"*The Ships a Sailing* laddie to *The Green Fields of America*
They'll take me o'er to *Bonnie Kate* who's my true *Cup of Tea.*

Then *Off to California* went *The Cameronian*
For *The Reconciliation* with *The Maid That Dare Not Tell.*
"Now-that *My Love is in America!*" exclaimed your wan *Scotch Mary,*
"I'm free to *Tear the Calico* so *Touch Me if You Dare!*"
"*Come West Along The Road*," says she-to *Young Arthur Daly*—O
"*Wink and She'll Follow You*," *Moll Roe* said at *Black Rock.*
She has *Money in Both Pockets, Tartan Plaid* and *Yellow Stock–ings*—So
Let you *The Bloom of Youth* take on *The Flower of the Flock!*"

To *The Daisy Field* beyond *The Tap House* on *The Mountain Top,*
Down Among the Rushes went this *Pullet and the Cock,*
Then to *The Silver Spire* they eloped-on *The Road to Knock,*
In the Merry Days of Easter up *The Stony Steps* in shock.
Well *The Smiles and Tears of Erin* shone on this *Bonnie Highlander,*
The Roudledum left her and *Rakish Paddy* with a *Chor–us,*
Ah Surely! I got to dread-ing how they would *Pay The Reckoning,*
I woke up with *The Risin' Sun* on the fifth part of *The Groves.*

© *Fintan Vallely*

The Folk revival in Britain, like the Traditional music revival in Ireland, was a period of tremendous energy and boundless, heady highs. You were playing music and singing morning, noon and night, and there was a community out there who not only wanted to hear it, but thought well of you for doing it. And even the parents approved, turning a blind eye to the nocturnal rambles, the arriving home at dawn (if at all), and the endless travel. For it was all a good cause—'culture'. At the same time those who were involved in the heady days of the development of Pop were getting a hard time across the board. That was 'mindless junk'. They were wasting their lives with unsavory people in unspeakable venues.

All cultural values are confidence tricks, like 'morals' shifting from era to era and culture to culture. But it isn't important that nowadays most Folk and Traditional musics are simply a viable part of contemporary music choices, or that most recordings, even by top performers, have lost their uniqueness value. What matters is that so many people in the 1960s and 1970s got hooked on music-making and singing with such passion that their movement produced an immense amount of reinterpretation, tremendous performances, and wonderful resources in print and on recordings. But there were some casualties along the way—broken lives and health, ruined Civil Service careers, and abandoned religions. And not least abandoned songs which were so relentlessly worked over they surely will not surface with value for another century. One such was another Eric Bogle song, his 1972 *The Band Played Waltzing Matilda,* which dealt with the Australian Anzacs being slaughtered at the Gallipoli peninsula in Turkey from 1915-1916. Sheila Miller from Edinburgh finally got thoroughly sick of the ersatz stuff.

Bootlegging Bogle

(Air: 'The Band Played Walting Matilda')

Oh, when I was much younger I played the banjo
And I sang round the Folk Clubs of Scotland.
From St. Andrews to Ayr, from Dumfries to Thurso,
To fightin' I ne-er gave a thought, man.
But in seventy-four, when my conscience was clean
Far up in the North—Inverness saw a scene

Which began such a conflict as never was seen
And the whole thing began with a lassie.
This lass she sang 'Waltzing Matilda'
And the Highlands were hushed at the sound
Except for the whirrs of the tape recorders
As the copycats' spools turned around.

How well I remember when I first heard that song,
Realised I was on to a good thing.
It could bring fame and fortune, I cared not a whit
That I hadn't the voice for to sing it.
But I wasn't alone, for those tapes soon spread
And then others too took it into their heads
To use 'Waltzing Matilda' to make them some bread,
We all jumped up on the bandwagon;
And we massacred 'Waltzing Matilda'
With our banjos, keyboards and guitars,
Self deprecators, ambitious proclaimers,
We became the Folk Club superstars.

Oh, we were the first, but in time others came
And we all had a hand in the slaughter,
The tuneless, the tasteless, the drunk, the insane,
And not one asked the leave of the author.
And long did we squabble and long did we fight
To be the first to record it—the others to spite.
Each worked out their arrangement and tried copyright,
Never thought of the man who first wrote it.
So we all sang 'Waltzing Matilda',
And we wrangled and bickered and brawled,
Till breath by breath, we just sang it to death
And now nobody sings it at all.

'Waltzing Matilda', 'Waltzing Matilda',
Who'll listen to 'Waltzing Matilda' with me? …
Breath by breath … we just sang it to death,
And now nobody sings it at all.

© Sheila Miller

Part 2: Agricultural Affairs

The Ballad of Binder Twine

Agriculture was revolutionised in 1834 by McCormick's invention of the reaping machine which was able to cut cereal crops, tie them into bundles, and toss them out the back into neat lines where the fine, bould peasantry could gather them into stooks at their leisure. However, just as the nuclear power plants have trouble disposing of their leftovers, so the 'binder' produced waste material, not by the ton, but by the mile—in the form of the 'binder-twine' used to do the tying. To make matters worse, the baler was invented some time later, which proved a total revolution in agriculture, but produced even thicker toxic waste—baler twine. There are vast amounts of this substance in any agricultural community. In fact, in the EEC there was a writhing mountain of it which forced them in desperation to invent the rollup machine which compresses yet more vast quantities of hay or whatever into big wheels which, per number of straws of vegetation, uses less kilometres of twine.

Originally, twine was made from natural fibres and it degenerated out in the fields after about a year, or about 40 years inside, but now it is made of plastic and seems indestructible. And it's here to stay—just like the awful plastic bag. In desperation one day after he discovered he couldn't fit any more of it into the barn, but still hadn't the heart to burn it, Mícheál Marrinan from Co. Waterford sat down instead and wrote this digression on the theme to the air of 'Bould Thady Quill'.

***

The Ballad of Binder Twine

(Air: 'Bould Thady Quill')

There's one great invention it is my intention
In song for to mention so listen a while,
With mighty potential in fact it's essential
To carry it with you whatever your style.
For farming 'twas made but 'twill suit any trade,
It comes in three colours of simple design;
You can cut it to size when the need it arises,
This mighty invention they call Binder Twine.

It may be amusing to find me enthusing
This subject I'm choosing in verse and in rhyme,
But I think it a scandal the wheel and the candle
Had no song to praise them since they were designed;
They have wrote about engines of great complications,
There are thousands of books on Professor Einstein;
But I cannot relate to his complex equations,
I'd rather be praising the ould Binder Twine.

You've heard of the builders of Egypt's great Pyramids
How they struggled for ages on those steep inclines,
How those rocks of great tonnage they shifted with courage
And pushed them and shoved them 'till they were in line.
'Twas the slaves done the labour all chained up together,
With the weight of those chains sure they must have been cryin';
Oh they would have worked faster if only their masters
Had tied them together with light Binder Twine.

Now excuse my transgression but I have been digressin',
For I have a confession and it is no lie ;
Last year on the road between home and Listowel
Sure me fan belt gave o'er and me wife she did sigh.
Now they say for repairing this great complication
A good pair of tights sure 'twill do it just fine;
Ah but me wife didn't have hers on this sad occasion
So I had to replace it with ould Binder Twine.

One final dimension of this great invention,
'Tis used as prevention—by farmers for gates.
The cows they respect it and the crows they detect it
And never will cross it for fear of their fate.
For tying in a hound or for squaring out ground
Or for holding up trousers that are in decline,
Such versatile uses are surely exclusive
To that mighty invention they call Binder Twine.

This song can be heard on Mícheál Marrinan's album Between Miltown & Ennistymon. Information and other lyrics are on www.irishsongs.net.

(Schitheredee version of this song appears in the Appendix on page 236.)

Rural Ireland is full of the lore of the cattlemart, the 'grader', the fair or 'the ring'—whatever it might be called in any given place. 'Dalin' is the commercial side of rearing beasts, for many farmers the most enjoyable part of it, but no matter how good the creature might be, if a farmer is no use at bargaining then a bad price will be got on market day. On the other hand a good wheeler-dealer can sell anything to anybody, but especially to a mug, or somebody who's had one too many. Brian McGuinness, a forester, late of the bardic lands around Dungiven in Co. Derry, wrote song and verse prolifically, and no dogfight in his locality escaped the sometimes rusty razor of his observational powers. A neighbour's misfortunes in the cattle trade are the subject of this piece which has as much trivia of bovine lore in it as a four-year veterinary course. No fewer than twenty-one ailments of cattle are listed—that's if you include superstition. The air is that of 'In Belfast there is no hope, for that man they call the Pope'. Co. Derry singer and songwriter Francie Brolly is the source of Brian McGuinness' manuscript.

***

The Ballad Of Rangy Ribs

(Air: 'In Belfast there is no hope, for that man they call the Pope')

Patrick Kealy is my name and I'm not unknown to fame
For the many void ventures that I've made
In that land of craft and fraud where unwary feet have trod,
Euphemistically called the cattle trade;
And of Hereford or Ayrshire that have graced my humble byre
(And I've had them black and white and red and blue)
There's none sticks in my mind, or left me so far behind,
As that Rangy Ribs I bought from Micky Dubh.

On his failings to begin, he was rangy-ribbed and thin,
Ring-boned and reeking with the hoose.
He was fluked and timber-tongued and he shivered when he dunged;
He staggered like a drunkard on the booze.

27

He was tubered for a fact, pig-mouthed and humpy-backed,
The warble fly had paid a visit too.
Had there been a sale for lice, sure I'd have doubled up the price
On that Rangy Ribs I bought from Micky Dubh.

His hair was scarce and dry, he had ringworm round one eye
And his kidneys by 'red water' sorely tried.
You still could see the rings where excruciating strings
Of garlic to his tall were often tied.
He had neither breadth nor length, walked more by skill than strength,
And his hurdy bones the skin had broken through;
Dissipated and forlorn, there was but a single horn
On that oul' Rangy Ribs I bought from Micky Dubh.

Mick was anxious for the sale and he hurried on the deal,
Sure I should have copped on from the start.
As he sang his praise to me and outlined his pedigree
That from Rangy Ribs he was inclined to part.
But the bargain bein' struck, Mick handed out the luck,
And to the baste he bade a fond adieu.
I sure could make a pile if I possessed the style
Or could master half the gas of Micky Dubh.

Well, optimistic for a year, I nursed him till it was clear
That condition to his ribs would never cling.
The conclusion I came to—in fact the only thing to do—
Was to tart-him-up and sell him in the market ring.
So I groomed him up and down till the Tuesday came around,
I was up before the cock had even crew;
I washed and combed my hair, headed for Dungiven fair
With the Rangy Ribs I bought from Mickey Dubh.

I remember well the day that we topped the Shambles Brae,
Outside McKenna's pub he gave a roar,
And he arched his humpy back and stopped dead in his tracks,
As if to say "I've anchored here before".
There he stuck me in the street in the blinding rain and sleet,
The interest and the offers they were few;
For though they looked him up and down I think they took me for a clown
With thon ould Rangy Ribs I bought form Micky Dubh.

I was hurted in my pride and I cursed his mangy hide,
Though in my heart I knew I'd no excuse.
And so, crabbit, wet and late, when I drove him in the gate
I decided there and then to turn him loose.
Ever for himself to fend, on his own he could depend
For I swore on bended knee that I was through;
No more nursing would he get—from me or quack or vet—
That oul' Rangy Ribs I bought from Micky Dubh.

Though he lent but little grace or distinction to the place,
He was useful-at-times my wife would often say;
From that heap of bones and trash she'd often hang the weekly wash
When the upright from the line had blown away
And it was a common sight to see red, blue, green and white
Of jumpers, shirts and skirts and drawers and bloo—mers,
And when Auntie Jane had passed sure he flew them at half-mast,
That ould Rangy Ribs I bought from Micky Dubh.

Of the temperament that strays, he was often gone for days and days,
Impossible to keep in any bounds,
And when these times did transpire we would eagerly enquire
If the postman ever saw him on his rounds.
Word of Rangy's boat could come from places far remote
As Magilligan, Strabane and even Toome,
But though he was a total wreck, still we always welcomed back
That oul' Rangy Ribs I bought from Micky Dubh.

Well, he roamed from Derryard to snow-capped high Minard,
From the fertile fields of Feeny to the Pass,
From clover-clad Fincairn to the meadows of Drumsurn,
So he must have been a specialist in grass.
At the Ligavailon Pot, the B-Specials nearly shot
Him — battle-scarred he roamed through Terrydoo,
And Laurie Quigg, it's said, often scared the weans to bed
With that Rangy Ribs I bought from Micky Dubh.

He was often lame and maimed from injuries he'd sustained,
Yet Old Man Death for long he seemed to foil.
He'd been stuck for hours on end in pipes up through the Glen
And pulled from every sheugh in Templemoyle.

We saved him from a gate on the Ministry estate,
And I cursed the trouble that he put us to,
When he lost his last remaining horn in a row in Bradley's corn,
That Rangy Ribs I bought from Micky Dubh.

But still a mist comes o'er my eyes when I think of his demise,
And the circumstances under which he died;
From the chill November blast I had got him housed at last
And in the byre had him strongly tied.
I was on my nightly rounds before I threw the body down
As any careful man is like to do,
When I found him cold as clay, choked by Duffy's musty hay,
That ould Rangy Ribs I bought from Micky Dubh.

Now when Madge heard the news she trembled in her shoes.
I wondered if her heart would stand the blow
We neither ate nor slept, but an all-night vigil kept
And we waked him till the cock began to crow.
At the first grey streak of dawn, I pulled my waders on,
Though it galled my heart the task I had to do;
By what light the candle gave, I washed and soaped and shaved
That oul' Rangy Ribs I bought from Micky Dubh.

We buried him next day where the sunlight strikes the brae;
The neighbours came from many miles around
To pay their last respects—for you never know who's next—
And to help commit his body to the ground.
Where with willing pick and spade his last resting place was made
And his coffin gently lowered from the 'bru'
Evermore to be at rest; Duffy's hay had proved the test
Of that Rangy Ribs I bought from Micky Dubh.

All my efforts to be brave collapsed now by the grave,
And down my cheeks the scalding tears did roll.
In the spasms of my grief I was shaking like a leaf
And I wondered if ould Rangy had a soul.
And I prayed if it be so that grass knee-high would grow
In the land that misadventure drove him to.
He'd have no more cause to roam but for once would stay at home,
That old Rangy Ribs I bought from Micky Dubh.

© *Brian McGuinness estate. This song can be heard sung on Kevin Mitchell's Greentrax album I Sang The Sweet Refrain.*

Part 3: The Lives of the Smaller Creatures

THE WATERFORD BOYS

Bed and Breakfast joints used be the field leaders in the bungalow bliss of rural Ireland north and south. Once upon a time they were no more than perfectly efficient living spaces, sometimes extensive in layout, but now, in tandem with developing architectural skills, they have sneaked upward, smuggling in roofspace rooms past the planners' regulations as 'dormer' bungalows. In these establishments you hear Radio 2FM perpetually; you discover the true meaning of chipboard, fabulous patterns of wallpaper, cream paint, autumn leaf carpet, inferior sprung mattesses and nylon bedspreads; you find out all the news about the proprietors and their children (none of whom you know and none of whom you will ever meet), their holidays, weddings, diseases and, thanks to confession radio, their most tedious secrets. You also get to eat what in the North is called an 'Ulster Fry', in the Republic an 'Irish breakfast', in Scotland a 'Scottish breakfast', and in England an 'English breakfast'— basically a cocktail of various metamorphoses of pig-meat, flour and grease, flavoured with plastic capsules of marmalade and washed down with tea or (instant, cleverly disguised by a pot) coffee. This must be consumed between the hours of 8 am and 10 am while under siege from the landlady who sits with her elbows on the table triumphantly blitzing you with nosiness and trivia. It is said that hoteliers invented the B&B to create a demand for their own discreet services. Before the days of either, inns did the job perfectly well, producing a welter of colourful songs in the process. This one is of the rat variety.

***

The Waterford Boys

For fun and diversion we have met together,
I tell you from Waterford hither we came;
We-e crossed the big ocean in dark stormy weather,
Our hearts they were light and our pockets the same.
Sad at leavin' old Ireland, we w're once more on drier-land,
By the roadside a tavern I chanced for to spy;
And as I was meltin' me pockets I felt in,
For the price of a drink I was mortally dry.

CHORUS:
For we are the boys with the Fol-de-dol eloquence,
Drinking and dancing and all other joys,
For ructions, destructions, diversions and divilment
Who's to compare with the Waterford boys?

In the tavern I rolled in and the landlord he strolled in.
"Good mornin'," says he, and says I "If you please—
Will you give me a bed and then bring me some bread
And a bottle of porter and a small piece of cheese?"
My bread and cheese ended, I then condescended
To seek my repose, sure I bid him, "Good night."
When under the clothes wher' I was goin' to doze
Sure I first popped me toes and then blew out the light.

Oh I wasn't long sleeping till I heard something creeping
And gnawing and chawing around the bedpost.
My breath I suspended but the noise never ended
Thinks I, "You have damnable class for a ghost."
For to make myself easy, I felt very lazy,
Me head once more I pulled out of the clothes.
"Yerra Jazes—what's that!"—didn't a great big jack rat
With one lep from the floor came right up to me nose.
CHORUS

Well, I reached for me hobnail and made him a bobtail
And wrestled with rats till the clear light of day,
When the landlord came in, and says he with a grin
"For your supper and bed you've five shillins to pay."
"Five shillins for what? Now don't be disgracin your— self"
Says I, "As a rogue if you please—
While I can't stay asleep with these rats, you've the Divil's own—
Grace for to charge me for dry bread and cheese."
CHORUS

Well the landlord went rarin' and leppin' and tearin,'
He jumped through the window and kicked in the door.
When he could get no further he roared at me with murder:
"These rats they are atin' me up by the score—
They sleep in me stable and eat from me table,
They wrestled me dogs and they've killed all me cats."
"In truth then," says I, "You'll give me these five shillin's,
And I'll tell you the way to get rid of the rats."
CHORUS

"An' I will then," says he. "Well, invite them to supper,
And dry bread and cheese lay before them, be sure;
Never mind if they're willin', but charge them five shillins,
And bad luck to the rats will you ever see more."

This song can be heard sung by Tim Lyons on his Green Linnet album
Easter Snow—Traditional Irish Songs (SIF 014, LP, 1978).

Tim Lyons has problems with the legless, eyeless, wriggling and fluid-transported, microscopic, anaerobic bastes in Miltown Malbay. But Con Ó Drisceoil experienced the Hammer House of Horror with the multi-limbed, self-propelled, aerobic variety. One night, long after he should have had more sense than to be lying out in a ditch (his forefathers and mothers having fought long and hard to get a roof over his head), he was *et* alive by clocks, earwigs, centipedes, spiders and wood-lice who had colonised his green, wholesome, natural-fibre sleeping bag. The following morning he was found scratched raw red, knocking up the chemist in quest of soothing swabs, unctions and drenches. After a few baths of baking soda he calmed down and could see that the creatures had meant him no harm, and were only doing their ecological duty. But he penned this defensive ballad to explain the intensity of his loathing of crawling things around tents.

***

The Miltown Cockroach

(Air: 'Trip to Gougane')

Oh, the west County Clare is a beautiful place,
Its people a charming and musical race,
'Tis pleasant to view it by car or by coach,
But a blot on the landscape's the Miltown Cockroach.
Rally ra, fol the day, rally ra fol the dee.

The Miltown Cockroach is a martyr for beer.
His eye it is evil, his aspect severe;
He barks like a bulldog and kicks like a mule,
And he drinks and he fights and plays games of pool.
Rally ra, fol the day, rally ra fol the dee.

In sweet Miltown Malbay one night in July
I retired to my tent as the sunrise was nigh;
Established in comfort with grunts and with yawns
I shortly was dreaming of tunes and *rabhcáns.*
Rally ra, fol the day, rally ra fol the dee.

But I woke with a start after two hours or so
To a loud crunching noise coming from my big toe.
This insect most foul then came into my view;
On the sole of my foot he continued to chew.
Rally ra, fol the day, rally ra fol the dee.

So, I jumped from the bag with a terrible screech
Saying, "Mister Cockroach, of the law you're in breach.
On a citizen's blood you may not slake your thirst
Without gaining the donor's approval at first."
Rally ra, fol the day, rally ra fol the dee.

"Of the legal position," says he, "I have doubt,
For this blood is at least fifty-eight percent stout.
So stop quoting the law and lie down again quick
Till myself and my clan carry on our picnic."
Rally ra, fol the day, rally ra fol the dee.

So, I tried to sweet talk him with eloquent chat
Saying, "A gourmet like you should know better than that,
Look at my carcass—it's scrawny and tough
While of plump tender youths there are surely enough!"
Rally ra, fol the day, rally ra fol the dee.

Says the cockroach, "You speak like a poet and a sage,
But truly you don't taste too bad for your age.
My friends have decided that here we will dine;
While the meat isn't great sure the pickle is fine."
Rally ra, fol the day, rally ra fol the dee.

So, since I'd failed with the brain then I opted for brawn;
We struggled and tore at each other till dawn.
I fought them with bites, head-butts, closed fists and kicks;
I tried burning and drowning and all sorts of tricks.
Rally ra, fol the day, rally ra fol the dee.

But those Draconian offspring came at me in gangs
With snarls and displaying their venomous fangs.
They crawled from the ditches and out of the sewers,
Ten thousand or more of them six-legged hoors.
Rally ra, fol the day, rally ra fol the dee.

They covered the ground like a black plastic sheet
Till I knew it was time to sound up the retreat.
I turned tail and ran, full of loathing and dread
And from sweet Miltown Malbay that morning I fled.
Rally ra, fol the day, rally ra fol the dee.

Oh, the Black Widow Spider is not a nice toy
And the African cobra is one ugly boy,
But both of them surely are cuddly and fair
Compared to the man-eating cockroach from Clare.
Rally ra, fol the day, rally ra fol the dee.

On July 17th, 1983, during one scorching summer, a Loggerhead turtle came ashore for its holidays at Quilty, Co. Clare thinking it had arrived at Shangri La. Witnessed by thousands of sun-stroked musicians, its size and colourings, its pedigree and species, age and nationality, all changed by the hour in direct proportion to the units of ultra-violet radiation absorbed and alcohol consumed. Eventually there was nothing for the turtle to do but to take to Guinness, so fond had it become of music and all the attention. And so it ended up, like everyone sooner or later, in Tom Queally's pub (a dangerous piece of fate-tempting for an already-endangered species, for Tom is also an undertaker). Within twenty four hours there were two songs written about it, both by people who had never seen it, a testament to local faith in the oral tradition. While Dubliner Antaine O'Farachán scribbled away at his version in Marrinan's, Ciarán Ó Drisceoil from Ballintemple, Co. Cork produced this one in Queally's; it appeared in the Clare Champion a couple of weeks later.

***

The Quilty Turtle

(Air: 'Preab san Ól')

In the Caribbean was to be seen
Once a turtle heading for Erin's isle;
It was his one dream to take the Gulf Stream
And get to Miltown for a while.
'Twas kind of chancy, but he'd heard of Clancy,
Of the danger he cast no thought;
And things were goin' great for seven months or eight
Till in a trawler's net he was caught.

This turtle splendid he was upended,
A rope tied round his enormous shell,
Much against the wishes of these satellite fishes
Who saw that things were not going well.
Off they did hurtle and left the turtle
Tied to the quay at the Seafield pier,
He was four foot eight and three hundred weight
With a pinkish spot behind the ears.

37

That night the turtle some girls did startle
When people thought that he was tied secure;
He slipped his moorings, ran down some boreens,
Stole a coat and trousers from behind a door.
He hitched a Citroen right up to Miltown,
Sat on a high stool in Queally's bar.
Said a girl called Úna, "Tis Ciaran MacMathúna
Or some other famous television star."

Twelve pints or more and he hit the floor,
Then in the parlour doorway his shell got jammed,
Where 'twas the fashion to attend the session
Although the parlour was already crammed.
Said Noel Hill, "Now I've had my fill,"
And tried to exit into the bar;
On the beast's abdomen he stepped when comin'
And in a minute there was holy war.

Well, he saw red then, that loggerhead gent,
And swallowed Hill in a single gulp;
A young flute player, one swipe did slay her;
He crushed Nick Adam's pipes to pulp.
There was no-one sounder to smash a counter,
Break glass and bottles when in the fray.
He ate a bodhrán and Jimmy O'Brien Moran,
Before the Gardaí came to save the day.

Taken back to Quilty, he was found guilty
Of bein' drunk and quite disorderly.
There was consternation at his deportation,
He was dropped by helicopter into the sea.
Here's to the turtle who swam the Gulf Stream
And drinks as much as a shark or whale;
With twelve pints of Guinness, no man is sinless,
And may we live long to tell the tale.

*'Preab San Ól' can be heard sung by Luke Kelly and Ronnie Drew on the dreaded
YouTube.com; also Seán de hÓra can be heard singing it on the more ostentatious
www.smithsonian globalsound.org*

As a child in "the good old days" I was brought up in a house with leaky doors and a mixture of mud and stone walls. These were riddled with a labyrinth of tunnels behind the plaster. Loose mortar permitted rat-runs that were impossible to trace, and so we were always over-run with the grey menace in winter-time. To combat this we perpetually maintenanced several branches of a centagenerational extended cat family, but since these preferred baby rabbits and robins, traps became both our final solution and childhood memory. The best of these was the steel variety (made in Germany, of course), but far more effective was the terrifying "DAK"—a gooey glue onto which the creature was lured by a bait, got stuck, rolled itself in a death-throe mess before finally perishing of terror or suffocation, all prior to, or as well as, being incinerated. In those far-off days before cement, there could be no mercy with mice: either you got them or they got you. This tale comes from the collecting and singing of Sean Corcoran.

***

The Mice Are At It Again

(Air: 'Trippin' up to Claudy')

Well, since we've lost our ould tomcat with mice we're over-run.
I've ordered traps in by the gross and poison by the ton.
I put my Sunday trousers on last night to make a show,
But as soon as I got on the street I said, "Hello! What O?"
The mice are at it again, as sure as bees is bees,
They're in and out the early doors and they're skitterin' round me knees.
I try to preserve my wardrobe but still it's all in vain,
For as soon as I find the drop behind—the mice are at it again.

Last week I earned some overtime and like a big fat head
I hung my trousers at the foot when I got into bed,
And the next morning when I awoke I found I had been done.
I asked the Missus about it and she says, "It's ten to one—that
The mice are at it again, bein' up to their tricks."
I said, "They must've been hungry for to chaw up seven and six,
For I knew I had half a sovereign!" "That's right!" says Mary Jane,
"And they chawed it down to half a crown—the mice are at it again!"

For to wash my neck I keep some whiskey round the place;
The bottle it is empty every mornin' I can trace,
I asked the old landlady who'd been drunk the night before,
Or did she know where my whiskey went and she says, "Dear O Lord!
O, the mice are at it again! Oh isn't it a shame!
For every night that I get tight, the mice they do the same.
I noticed a couple this morning, they were tryin' to cool their brains
They were run in about with their tongues hangin' out —
Oh! The mice are at it again!"

While waitin' at a bus-stop a lady says to me,
"You are just the saucy surgeon I've been waitin' for to see."
Her voice was full of whiskey and her manner full of grace,
But as soon as she lifted up her veil, I said, "Is that a face?"
For the mice were at it again! Talk about a clock!
For when I saw it in the lamp, it gave me quite a shock.
I said, "Fare thee well, Old Solomon, your dial would stop a train,
So take it away and boil it, for the mice are at it again!

Sean Corcoran can be heard singing this song on Sailing Into Walpole's Marsh, download from www.emusic.com.

Part 4: Bejasusbetterin'

1783: "…What little the men can earn by their labour, or the women by their spinning, is generally consumed in whiskey… Shoes and stockings are seldom worn by these beings who seem to form a different race from the rest of mankind; their poverty is far greater than that of the Spaniards, Portuguese, or even the Scotch peasants; notwithstanding which, they wear the appearance of content." 7

1836: "The poor Irish work merely for their support; for what can, at the lowest calculation, sustain life…Beyond this their degraded condition does not permit them to pass. To hold out to such people a prospect of support…might prove injurious in the highest degree." 8

1839: "But they are generally happy; therefore why wish to alter their state?"9

1846: "An Irishman commits a murder as a Malay runs a-muck. " 10

1847: "The English are naturally industrious—they prefer a life of honest labour to one of idleness… of all the Celtic tribes, famous everywhere for their indolence and fickleness… the Irish are admitted to be the most idle and the most fickle. " 11

"Irish people! poor creatures, it is quite amusing to hear them thus dignified by being supposed to take an interest in the stormy discussions in the House of Commons."12

1849-51: "You can trace the descent in their blighted, stunted forms—in their brassy, cunning, brutalised features… Their huts… monuments to national idleness… the missing link between the gorilla and the Negro."13

"The very name [Ireland] forces to our recollections images of shillelaghs, and broken heads, and turbulence of every kind"[14]

And then the ungrateful bastards had the audacity to rise up and bite off the gentle hands which penned these generous profiles. The poor and dispossessed, the marginal groups in any society not only have the *lavins* of the table but then become the butt of its wit too. Mother-in-laws and wives have been the subjects of much humour in the past, but now the concepts aren't even considered funny, such has been the educative power of the ideology of feminism (the odd kick in the balls helped too). Living midst eviction and poverty in Ireland, or in the overcrowding and human degradation of the boom-towns and ports of nineteenth century Industrial England, the Irish as an underclass behaved often as their status determined. Society outside could observe from the safe distance created by that double stigma of poverty and Irishness—and laugh at the antics. Travelogues told of the sub-species back on the island; cartoons depicted them and their political leaders crudely and vividly. Through a dozen or more successive generations, the cumulative psychological effect of the media and political barrage effected a genetic mutation on the British mind, still in evidence by the 1990s in Unionist, Colonial-minded politicians like John Taylor who famously cited the difference between Protestants and Catholics as being 'we don't dance at crossroads'. The Stage Irishman arose out of this, first depicted by Samuel Lover as 'Handy Andy'—a handy capsule to contain and dispense political intolerance of the Irish. The same ideas—racism—exist in the all-white European ex-Colonial societies today, still demonstrated by jokes about Poles and Jews. 'Nigger' jokes have been obliterated by black political action and its educative effect (it scared the shit out of white people); American and Kerrymen jokes linger on to preserve the structure of the tiring humour genre. But as a figure the Stage-Irishman was unique—is still so, in British culture—and still galls Irish people abroad. Of 'Paddy', it has been most positively said that he offered the chance to scorn the creators of the image, by taking refuge in Him as a vehicle from which coded insult, understandable properly only to the Irish themselves, could be vented. This far into the Irish state, the biting insult of His image has been diluted, inside Ireland, into a far-off fond nostalgia, rehabilitating Him as almost 'all right'. Thus Cork poet Eoghan Denis can speak of addressing nobility with: "God bless you—sor", where 'sor' is the Irish for 'louse'.

Paddy wasn't always so pliant and accepting of his lot. The *No Irish Need Apply* notices bred their own level of resentment, some of which came out in song. A level-headed explanation of the situation follows.

***

Paddy's Lament

Oh, here I am from Donegal, I feel quite discontented
To see the way that we're run down and poorly represented,
For it seems it is a general rule
To make out Pat a knave or fool,
But never mind he'll play it cool, and stand up for old Ireland.

CHORUS:
So, do me justice, treat me fair, and I won't be lamentin',
And I won't be laughed at anywhere, but highly represented.

Now Mister Punch with his literature, he treats us very badly,
And when he draws our caricatures, depicts us rather sadly:
With crooked limbs and villainous face,
he thus portrays the Irish race,
We think it is a sad disgrace, and we say so in old Ireland.
CHORUS

When on the stage I do appear with thunderin' great shillelagh,
With ragged coat and tattered hat—You'd think I'd come out gaily—
With not a word of commonsense
They don't know when they give offence,
But carry on at Pat's expense, why don't they come to Ireland?
CHORUS

The 'Irish mother's letter to her son' we don't find witty.
The 'Irish GCE' and jokes all are the nitty gritty
Of racist prejudice at work ;
As with Asians, Jews, Blacks, Poles and Turks,
The deep-down hate is THAT we work tho' they call us 'lazy Ireland.'
CHORUS

They say we're dirty and lazy got, but what's the use to grumble?
For if they call in an Irish cot, they're welcomed though 'tis humble.
And in Public Works the country round
Or where hard work is to be found
In railway tunnels underground you'll find the boys from Ireland.
CHORUS

It's very true I like a glass, it makes me feel quite frisky,
And I'm very fond of an Irish lass, but I'm fonder of the whiskey.
I'm very quiet when left alone
But I do what I like with what's my own,
And woe betide the foes of home who'd dare run down old Ireland.
CHORUS

Roisín White can be heard singing this as 'Do Me Justice' on her album
The First of My Rambles. Verse 4 © Fintan Vallely

In 1805 John Carr related the following anecdote, describing the behaviour of a (probably mythic) Irishman who had come into money and decided to do the 'Grand tour' of the Continent:

"After passing through France and Italy, and part of Spain, with scarcely any emotions of delight, he entered a village in the latter country where he saw a mob fighting very desperately, upon which in a moment he sprang out of his travelling carriage without once enquiring into the cause of the battle, or ascertaining which side he ought in justice to espouse, he laid about him with his shilala, and after having had several of his teeth knocked out, and an eye closed, and the bridge of his nose broken, he returned to the carriage, and exclaimed, "By Jasus! it is the only bit of fun I have had since I left Ireland." [15]

A suitable introduction to the next song, which comes from the singing of Finbar Boyle from Dundalk. The air is, suitably, that of 'The Teetotaller' reel.

**

Invitation to a Funeral

(Air: 'The Teetotaller')

I got an invitation to go to a funeral,
But to my disappointment, sure, the fella didn't die.
He tould the undertaker he was vexed at disappointing us,
And if he'd apologise to us we'd let the thing go by.
To make up for disappointin' us, he brought us out and treated us;
He called for pints of porter for the company attending,
Until some fella questioned him whose money was he squanderin';
He put the fella's eyelids into mournin' there and then.

When the owner of the beershop saw a row a comin' on
He gave orders to evict us but of course we did refuse;
He whistled on some lodgers that were sittin' in the corner,
And for ten and fifty minutes we were badly abused.
When we left the beershop and down the streets a staggering,
A crowd of corner boys started peltin' us with mud.
We asked them to go aisy and they tould us they were doin' that,
Then we turned on them and left them lyin' where they stood.

45

The next thing we encountered was a party of Salvationers;
They rifled all our pockets and then asked if we were saved.
Wee Jon McGinty got escorted to the station house
For askin' a pol-iceman if his appetite was shaved.
To raise McGinty's bail we all took off our undershirts
And straight to the pawn shop we took the jolly lot:
We asked the man for ten and six, the price to free McGinty.
"He has had enough already," was the answer that we got.

But we got the ten and sixpence and went off to free McGinty.
But the devil take the beershop if it met us on the way!
And we couldn't pass the corner without havin' some refreshments,
And we spent every penny of the fine we had to pay.
We bought a concertina for to have the high hilarity,
None of us could play it, though we tried our best and worst.
We made enough noise with it, if that was any benefit;
We handled it so gentle that the bellows went and burst.

Then we bought some hot potatoes for to mend the concertina,
But someone hit Moloney with the carcass of a cat;
He buttoned up his whiskers and began to read the riot act
And swore he'd put two heads upon the divil who'd done that.
Moloney hit McCluskey and McCluskey hit some other man,
And everyone hit anyone to whom he owed a spite,
And the cripple McNamara who was sittin' saying nothin'
Got a crack that broke his eyes for not engagin' in the fight.

The drink had made us innocent, the sense was nearly out of us,
And for a bit of riotin' we quickly did prepare.
We battered one another till we weren't worth thr:ee ha'pence, and
I'm sure there was a carpet on the floor of skin and hair.
We battered left and right till the police separated us:
They marched us off to jail, broken noses and black eyes.
They locked us up in prison and for me it was a lesson, for
To never go to funerals until the people die.

This song can be heard on Rosie Stewart's album, Adieu to Lovely Garrison.

The North West of Ireland had a great flood of emigration to Scotland, and the connections which the counties Derry and Donegal have with Glasgow are intense. This is a song of the bigotry which often accompanied employment in the latter city in the end of the 19th century and the early part of the 20th. It rises well to the occasion, glorifying the pre-emptive, defensive action and temporary victory. And in case there is any doubt about who comes out best, even the filthy, louse-ridden barracks accommodation is converted to part of the victory plot and the dacent grub that we are supposed to have been reared on in Ireland gets full credit for the survival capacity of the labourer.

***

Round the Mickey Dam

I'm an honest Irish labourer
And I come from the county Derr—y,
Once I had a farm there
With nothin' much to share,
So I had to sell me donkey
And me famous Billy goat
And with the money that I got
To Glasgow got the boat.
On the mornin' when I landed there
Before me hair was dry
I was started in a Mickey Dam
In a place they call Mill-guy.

Now the ganger that I started with
They called him John the Mouse,
And the very first day that I was there
At me he made to grouse
But I quickly suprised him,
I said, "You little rat,
I'll tie a string around your neck
And I'll throw you to the cat;
For I'm as strong as any lion,
I was reared on eggs and ham,
I'm a terror to all fightin' men
Round the Mickey Dam."

Now this riz the Mouse's temper
And at me he made to jump.
He swore he'd paralyse me with
The handle of a pump.
But I quickly suprised him,
I grabbed him by the throat
And I shook that little monkey till
The tail came off his coat.
For I'm as strong as any lion
I was reared on eggs and ham,
I'm a terror to all fightin' men
Round the Mickey Dam.

Now the big hotels we're stoppin' in—
They call them navvy's huts—
And the bugs and fleas are in the beds
As big as coconuts;
On Saturdays when I come in
I hide behind the door
And as they come out one by one
I bash them to the floor.
For I'm as strong as any lion
I was reared on eggs and ham,
I'm a terror to all fightin men
Round the Mickey Dam.

Kevin Mitchell can be heard singing this on the Greentrax album I Sang The Sweet Refrain.

Part 5: Goatery And Percussion

At this stage everybody knows what a bodhrán (pronounced bough [as in bow-wow, doggie] -ran) is. During the 'Revival'—or re-popularisation of Irish traditional music—throughout the sixties and seventies, most of its devotees were content with the narcosis engendered by the combination of healthy young bodies, bursting sexuality, pints and pints of beer and the odd gaseous stimulant. But there was a mad stampede by others to get doing something musical. Many of these were innocent dabblers, and would sometimes take up the tin whistle. That was often considered to have no sex appeal and too hard, so more commonly they would take up the bodhrán.

This infatuation with simplicity is also one of the curious facts to emerge from observation of the music-loving species of foreign tourist in Ireland. Traditional music is played on many and varied instruments—flutes and concertinas that were made in the 19th century, accordions from all over Italy, sets of pipes decorated in silver, gold and elephant that cost thousands of pounds... yet nothing will do even the most sophisticated Music Tourist but they'll have to get their hands on a bodhrán —a piece of a dead goat's skin nailed onto an old bit of bent plywood that isn't even unique to Ireland. Some say that the primitive thump could be felt to mimic the pounding machinery of the Teutonic work-ethic, but, whatever it is, it has created a glut of bodhráns on the market. Worse still, it has made the life of an Irish goat about as relaxed as Salman Rushdie's.

The use of the bodhrán is not exactly an ancient tradition in Ireland, and it does not seem to have been either too serious or widespread; in only one picture of Irish musicians from the 19th century period does percussion of this nature appear. Nor is it mentioned in literature much (neither, mind you, are mouth organs, Jew's harps or tin whistles which were played widely at the time). All indications are that Irish music is primarily a melodic tradition, with perhaps rigid time foot-tapping and dancing fulfilling the percussive role. This is verified by the 1980s boom in 'sets' (revived 18th century, French parlour-dancing) rather than bodhrán-playing as they might have done in the sixties. Vertical percussion, *mar a dhea*. Musicians content themselves with the delusion that this is a wholesome traditional thing to be doing ("tunes were designed to be danced to", etc., etc. and other contrived, romantic rubbish), but if they realised that these set dancers were bodhrán players in disguise the music would stop. In any case, several hundred goats per annum give their lives in pursuit of the bodhrán fashion, and tonnes of the devices are played by otherwise vegetarians. All other aspects of traditional music are at the worst wilfully self-destructive and involve no bloodshed or harm to any other creature.

Scorned with curlèd lip by Traditional music's most revered authority, Breandán Breathnach, the bodhrán and its re-invention coincided with the international revived fashion in Folk musics, and this drum, multiplying in geometric progression, in Ireland and England at least, has become a Josserite[16] symbol of instant access to the music-making process. It has reached nonsense proportions in the Irish Fleadh Cheoil and English Folk Festival scene where a humming roomful of fresh purchases is often to be experienced. In these circumstances, a melody instrument may well start off the music, but the percussion swells in and eventually becomes an end in itself, giving the melodicist a chance to get to the chemist for aspirin.

Anybody from Europe who visits West Clare always goes first to Doolin, earning them all the title "Vasindoolins"—derived from the typical gushing reply to the question "How are you?"[17]. But in fact if it wasn't for tourism, people in the West would either be in America, or else poverty-stricken and utterly depressed. How else could they have the chance of such emotional release as being able to rip the back of people loudly, in public and without fear? With tourism rampant, there are enough of the rainbow-hued, nylon-zipped, alcohol-free, self-sufficient masochists around to create a summer-long carnival of gutting and sneering, and, on a wet day when they are plentiful, the pleasure may even be generously shared out with the native tourists from Dublin and Belfast who foolishly consider the gesture an intimacy and a great privilege. A standard observation in the Folk-rip catalogue is that the typical Music Tourist believes a glass of Guinness to be the ticket into the session, so explaining why insipid glasses of stout are hugged by those people for hours on end while waiting for the session to begin, unaware that all the time the session is the natives roaring and shouting all around them, heroically swilling porter by the gallon (on the last day of the Willie Week in 1990 Tom Queally sold 900 pints of Guinness alone). The MT's s are in the *Guinness Book of Records* both for taking the longest time to drink a glass of Guinness, and for wearing yellow wellies the longest after the age of four and a half. Indeed it is the absurdity of that very Wellington fashion that prompts Leitrim writer Brian Leyden to remark that only continental types wear them on the holidays—Irish people wouldn't be seen dead in them.

Whatever about all that, bodhráns are, for some reason, loathed and pompously despised, and have a whole genre of pseudo-sanctamoniousness built up around them which includes jokes:

—The best way to play them? (with a penknife, blowlamp)

—The difference between a good pair of brogues[18] (or a Radox Foot Spa™[19]) and a bad bodhrán player? (One of them bucks up your feet)

—If you found three bodhrán players buried up to their necks in sand what conclusion would you come to? (One for more sand.)

—A man leaves a large parcel beside a fiddle-player in a Belfast session. "What's in that?" the fiddler says nervously. "Semtex"[20] is the reply. "Oh, that's all right," says the fiddler. "I thought it might be a bodhrán."

—A man buys a stuffed rat in an antique shop. Out on the street he is followed by a horde of rats. Panic-stricken he heads for the pier, throws in the rat and they all dive in after it and so perish. Back he goes to the shop: "Eh— you wouldn't by any chance have a stuffed bodhrán player?"

—The difference between a bodhrán-player and a hedgehog, both killed on a road? (The hedge-hog's the one with the skid-marks in front of it.)

—The difference between a bodhrán and an onion? (Nobody cries when the skin is taken off a bodhrán.)

—How do you know a bodhrán player's at the door? (The knock speeds up.)

Before the bodhrán was invented these remarks were directed at guitar players (best way to play it—with wire cutters), before that at accordion players (back to the pen-knife again)[21] and nowadays at concertina classes (Chinese lantern workshops). In America too, cartoonist Gary Larsen has started a fad of so molesting banjo players, and Nancy Groce has a wonderful book of anti-musician jokes. The only other aspect of the bodhrán not dealt with here is its use by Ireland soccer football fans to accompany the complex 4/4 tribal melodies "O Lay, O Lay, O Lay, O Lay" (an ethnic egg-farmer's lullaby) and "Here we go, here we go, here we go" (traditional potty-training song).

This song started out life as an introduction to Tim Lyons', but gradually took on a purpose of its own. As the Killorglin Review of Bodhránabilia (ed. J.B. Keane) said: "The work substantiates the classic paradox often posed by the antinomies resonating within the Irish Traditional instrumentalists' experiential domain." Everybody loves to hate bodhrán players.

**

Confessions of a Bodhrán Player

(Air: 'Ould Rigadoo, Jolly Beggarman')

I'm a new-age vegetarian, Greenpeace-y sort of chap;
I save my whales and, as a male, I don't indulge in sexist crap;
I eat brown rice and bread—instead of bacon, meat and chops.
I dress in 'Threads', sleep in 'Futon' beds and I don't talk — I 'Rap'.
Now this lifestyle's most appealing, and by all the outward signs
I've left the structured feelings of consumer life behind;
But I'll confess that I've a failing that I can't control, I find
I need percussion's healing beat to regulate my mind.

CHORUS:
Rup, rup, ruppety buppety ruppety buppety bup
Ruppetty buppety ruppety buppety
Ruppety, bup, bup, bup …

So you might want to know why don't I have a go at flutes,
Rebabs or Balalaikas, Saz, Gadulkas, Lyres or Lutes—
But the ruthless, brutal truth I'll put—I couldn't give a hoot,
If I can't pluck, pick bow, strum, squeeze, sing, yo-dell, tinkle, rasp or toot.
For I have a basic problem with an ideolog'cal root—
Factory instruments on principle I must refute.
So the Bodd—Ran[22] hue-d from bended woo-d,
A goatskin, nails and glue is the closest thing to nature that in style
    —and price—will do,
CHORUS

And yes, I know it's con-tra-dict-ry—I'm exploiting a goat's hide—
For leisure, when all other leather yokes I won't abide,
But I just close my ears to pressure from the slashers who would thrash me
For bashing it with pleasure even after it has died.
Yes, I'm happy just to wallop time with others of like mind,
While intol-er-ant mel-od-i-cists are pompously unkind
With their smart-ass, smug pre-ten-tious-ness, guffaws, and glib pis-eogs,[23]
About 'Semtex', 'Onions', 'Hedgehogs', 'Foot-spas', 'Sand', 'Rats',
    'Pen-knives' and 'Brogues'.
CHORUS

So, truthfully I'd rather have us gathered in some room
With 'Weatherglazing' cladding, to preserve our sonic boom
Where we'd lather up the batteries, like a mighty Samba school,
And raise a Harvey Smith to all self-righteous ethnic rules.
So yous Ugandans, Turks, Nigerians, Afghanis, Sikhs, Ghan-ese,
Hindustanis, Pakistanis, Jap-pa-pan-ies, Indo-nese—
You can shove your Talkin' Drums, your ould Tablas, Kotos
    and Tarambukas—
We can do it better on our instrumental Pookas.[24]
CHORUS

Farewell, Mustapha Tettey Addy[25], and Ye Drummers of Burundi,
Ye Lambeg-totin' Paddies, Sabri Brothers and Donal Lunny,
Mel, Ringo, Colm, John-Joe, Cathy, Tommy, Kevin Coneff,
Any bum can thump for fun—and be an instant drummer.
So come all ye music dreamers who're orig'nally eccentric,
Buy a Bodd Rán—and it seems that you're indig'nously authentic.
But if Ó Riada could "phone home" he might say he "hadn't really
    meant it"— "Yet
If the Bouwrán hadn't been around—some fucker would invent it."
CHORUS

© *Fintan Vallely. This can be heard on* Big Guns and Hairy Drums.

Ever aware of this scenario all round him the whole summer long, Tim Lyons tells the original yarn about the bodhrán in song. In this he lets the goat get away, thus protecting the sensitive virtual musician from a pounding headache. Sensibly enough he robbed 'The Cuckoo's Nest' to lay his tonic eggs in—in an attempt to eliminate the possibility of any singer ever learning the song.

***

The Bodhrán Song

(Air: 'The Cuckoo's Nest' —three part)

Oh, me name is Heinrich Schnitzel
And from Germany I do come,
Of all the music in the world
I much do like the drum.
These last days I've been to Irelant
Where musicianers play till dawn.
It was there I meet and fell in love
With a drum they call "BOH-RAWN".

One day I'm going to Doolin famed
In music, song and dance,
And as I did hug my Fürstenberg
My mind was in a trance,
For there behind two whistles
In between a box and flute
A thunderous bang, and a goaty whang,
The air it did pollute.

This hairy drum my mind did numb,
In love with it I fell.
And I strongly did desire one
Despite the awful smell.

54

Enquiries then I soon did make,
Me mind being sorely bent
As to why and when and where and how
I'd procure such instrument.

I approached this bodhrán driver now
Being drunken with the sound:
"To purchase one of these yokes
Will cost you fifty pounds."
My mind did race at a gross pace
About my wallet thick.
He then did roar "SIXTEEN POUNDS MORE—
FOR CANVAS BAG AND STICK!"

"Oh mein gotten!" I'm exclaiming now,
"This is most expensive loot:
At home ve are not paying this
For a silvery concert flute."
"It isn't likely known", says he,
"And I don't give a hoot, but
Why don't you lend a gun from off some-one
And your own goat you can shoot?"

Now this seemed to me a bright idea
And became my sole intent,
For we German ones are good with guns
And brainy to invent.
Off I went without delay
And a shotgun I did borrow,
Says I, "I'll haff my goatskin now
This evening or tomorrow."

So upon the Burren mountain top
I stealthily did creep
O'er its craggy hill tops,
Into its valleys deep,
When there suddenly appeared to me
A herd of ragged goats
With horns high and yellow eye,
Great manes and shaggy coats.

As they thundered by I then let fly
Me Ely's Number 5.
When the smoke had cleared
It soon appeared
These goats were still alive.
I pursued them with alacrity
Till me legs were nearly lame;
But in vain I stood, it was no good,
Back to Doolin then I came.

And as I walked up by Fisher Street,
My spirits dragging low,
I heard a thick and a heavy voice
Cry out, "HALLO, HALLO!
I observe a deadly weapon—
Pray, tell me, is it your own?
Where is the licence for this gun—
To me it must be shown."

"Oh to plainly tell the truth to you
Nix licence have I got,
For I just borrowed it from Gerry Smith
To have a sporting shot."
"GER SMITH! HOW DO! I'm arresting you,
A subversive you must be
From some revolting movement
In far off Germany."

So now I lie in Ennis jail
Lamenting my condition;
The jury found me guilty,
Ten pounds fine and extradition.
The sergeant swore me life away,
The judge he called me barmy,
Said, "You're a Baader Meinhoff refugee
And a member of the Red Army."

So farewell to Ireland's fields of green
Far famed in song and poem,
Farewell to Burren's rocky slopes
Where wild bodhráns do roam;
If ever I return again
I'll shoot no goat or kid,
And when I want to bate me drum
I'll pay up me fifty quid.

© Tim Lyons. This can be heard on the album Big Guns and Hairy Drums.

There is a magical landscape overhanging the Summer Isles in the vicinity of the Tolkienesque Staic Polly, north of the port of Ullapool in top-leftern Scotland. Back in 1988, following a whisky and prawns gig in Andy Wilson's Fúarán Bar at Achiltiebuie, our roadie, Brian O'Rourke, succumbed to a state of unconsciousness which we attributed to an excess of Ian Campbell's seductive malt. Under cover of his silence, and relaxed in the freedom from his perpetual chimney-fire, pea soup emissions, Tim Lyons plotted out the course of a song about the bodhrán drum—from the point of view of the goat. He thought nothing more about the brain-wave until after that night's gig in the King Hakin bar on Skye, when Brian presented us with the full song, the idea for which had come to him in a dream. A coup was a coup: later, Tim wrote the German version, and Brian eventually recorded this, the Achiltiebuie one.

***

When I Grow Up
(Air: 'In Belfast There is No Hope')

Oh I am a year-old kid, I'm worth scarcely twenty quid,
I'm the kind of beast that you might well look down on;
But my value will increase at the time of my decease,
For when I grow up I want to be a bodhrán.

If you kill me for my meat, you won't find me very sweet,
Your palate I'm afraid I'll soon turn sour on;
Ah, but if you do me in for the sake of my thick skin,
Then you'll find I'll make a tasty little bodhrán.

Now my parents, Bill and Nan, they do not approve my plan
To become a yoke for every yob to pound on;
But sure I would sooner scamper with a bang than with a whimper
And achieve re-incarnation as a bodhrán.

I look forward to the day when I can leave off eating hay
And become a drum to entertain a crowd on;
And I'll make my presence felt with each well-delivered belt
As a fully manufactured concert bodhrán.

For when I'm killed then I'll be cured, and my career will be assured,
I'll be a skin you'll see no scum or scour on;
But with studs around my rim, I'll be sounding out the tim—bre
And I'll make a dandy, handy little bodhrán.

Oh! My heart with joy expands when I dream of far-off lands
And consider all the streets that I will sound on;
And I pity my poor ma who was never at a Fleadh
Or indulged in foreign travel as a bodhrán.

Now all sorts of cats have nine—lives, and they may well be fine,
And dogs I think have not too much to growl on;
But it's when you are a goat that you can strike a merry note,
Provided you have first become a bodhrán.

For a hornpipe or a reel a dead donkey has no feel,
Or a horse or cow or sheep that has it's shroud on;
And you can't join in a jig as a former Grade A pig
But you can wallop out the lot if you're a bodhrán.

So if ever you feel low, to a session you should go
And bring me there to exercise an hour on;
And you can strike a mighty thump on my belly, back or rump,
But I'd thank you if you'd wait till I'm a bodhrán.

And when I dedicate my hide, I'll enhance my family's pride
Tradition is a thing I won't fall down on;
For I'll sire a few young kids who'll be glad of the few quid
That they'll get for their ould lad to make a bodhrán.

Now I think you've had enough of this rubbishy ould guff,
So I'll put a sudden end to this wee amhrán,[26]
And quite soon my bleddy bleat will become a steady beat
When I start my new existence as a bodhrán.

This song can be heard on Brian O'Rourke's album When I Grow Up.

On a visit to Peadar Ó Doirnín mystic country for the magnificient October Forkhill Singers' weekend some years later, Liverpudlian Fred McCormick, a noted authority on the Irish language, took a dislike to Brian O'Rourke for misrepresenting the thoughts of an intelligent kid. After all, wouldn't only an eegit want to be a bodhrán? And are not goats an intelligent, highly-evolved species? Eventually he pushed the topic over the fine line which separates pub-talk from PhD research, and his effort will no doubt generate a couple of years of layabouting to occupy some unemployed American student who doesn't want to ever grow up to do a dacent day's work.

***

The Goat's Reply

(Air: 'In Belfast There is No Hope')

I'm a poor downtrodden kid from whom justice has been hid,
Whose head threats constantly rain down on;
For my loftiest ambitions face parental opposition,
And I'm told I'm only fit to be a bodhrán.

My parents, Nan and Bill, have tried to subjugate my will.
To force my hand they've turned the verbal power on;
But I would rather go with the divil that I know
Than wind up in Düsseldorf a lonely bodhrán.

My noble kith and kin bequeathed me a gentle skin,
It's the kind you'd pour the Chanel number five on;
And I would surely love to be a handbag or kid glove:
There's lesser bastes well fit to be a bodhrán.

There are elephants galore, tigers, gnus, giraffes and boars,
Dogs, llamas, wildebeests, gazelles and lions.
If the fishes in the sea were utilised instead of me
You could play a rake of scales upon a bodhrán.

A subscription I will pay now to the ISPCA
To keep me from the paws of any moron
Who, the moment I have died, will stretch and tan my hide
And wallop my backside as a new bodhrán.

Now I'd have no objection if I'd choice in resurrection,
I'd return as fiddle, flute or an accordion;
For with my luck some tuneless shit, or mindless thumpin' German git,
Will possess me if I end up as a bodhrán.

If the glories of the Celt depend on belt and bang and welt,
On a baste that's long deceased, then I'd call down on
The entire Irish race humiliation and disgrace,
With special doses for the ones who're making bodhráns.

But there's bards and kings and chiefs, there's elaborate motifs,
There's a language that's served many's a fine *amhrán;*
There's Beckett, Yeats and Joyce, you can easy take your choice:
Any none of those you bet would bate the bodhrán.

I've often heard it said that a drum should have two heads
And I'll bet there's some with three or four on;
But how many goats have died for a drum with just one side?
You're not just dead meat, but incomplete, when you're a bodhrán.

So I hope I've said enough in this elaborate rebuff,
And I've given drummers guilty thoughts to drown on;
Goats won't have peace of mind till there's no value on their rind
When humanity abolishes the bodhrán.

© *Fred McCormick*

61

Related to the bodhrán, but a different concept altogether, is the Lambeg drum. Contrary to the way the Different Drums ensemble are fooling around with the device in the company of bodhráns and djembes at the moment, the relationship lies only in the source for the skin—a goat. Wilbert Magill, a councillor from Newtownards, Co. Down, is adamant that the choice of goat is crucial, and a good goat could therefore be being sized up from behind a hedge over a period of time, unaware that it was to be the victim of eventual summary execution to further the cause of political percussion. A nanny is what is desirable for the lambeg skin, and preferably an unblemished white one at that. None of your spotty hides that are fashionable among hard-men bodhrán players and which make the thing look as if it was made from a piebald pony, and none of your old bits of hair left hanging pubic-style on to the side. Nor does the Lambeg maker want his goat to have had a colourful history—such as might be associated with a Billy goat. Bill's adventures typically take him through thorn hedges, sloe bushes, barbed wire fences, holes in stone walls and old bedspring gaps; his misdemeanours earn him beatings with sticks and stones, shotgun pellets and murderous attacks by razor-toothed alsatians. In short, his skin, ravaged too by all sorts of vermin, is only fit for a bodhrán. With the large expanse required by a Lambeg, the high tension used in its construction (and caused by its application), the forces applied in its exercise (exaggerated by shrinkage on a hot day), the essential that it not split if struck by the player at a slightly imperfect angle—all demand a perfect skin. And so the next song is a combination of simple necessity (where a request would have been out of the question anyway), and a political blow being struck, so to speak. This was sung by Richard Hayward;[27] the air is that of *The Old Orange Tree*.

***

The Papish Goat

(Air: 'The Old Orange Tree')

In the County Down close to Seaforde town
All at Drumaness did dwell;
An oul' rogue there, you would compare
With the minor Judge of Hell.

Sure on Rogan's Rocks he does feed his flocks
And he had a goat last year
That was three years oul' so I've been toul'
And he loved that goat most dear.

Sure this oul' ceogh boy he got up one day
With his goat some pence to earn,
Nor little he thought of the gunk he'd get
When the cruel truth he'd learn.
For the Orangemen had been round that night,
You may guess what he did say
When the horns and the flesh of the goat lay there
But the hide had gone away;

Sure he ran hotfoot to the Seaforde town
And to the Squire he did say:
"Sir, some Hell's kin my goat did skin
And your rent I cannot pay."
And that gentleman he began to laugh
Till he drove the oul rogue mad,
And he let a howl and he swore by his soul
He would have him off Drumsnad.

And he came to mind of a boast they'd made
When they walked on the last Twelfth day
That they'd head their drum with a Papish hide
For the 'Protestant Boys' to play;
And he let a shout, just like Hell come out,
And a bad word did he say
Till his rage grew wild and like a child
He could neither curse or pray.

And when that to his home returned
Sure his cries would cleave the sky
Saying, "They never will have luck, for the skinnin' o' me buck
Till the day they droop and die."
But on the Twelfth day of July
It does drive him nearly dumb
For to hear the sound of a Papish goat
On the head of their Orange drum.

Part 6: Condomania

Prior to 1983 the sale of contraceptives was illegal in Ireland. You took your chances with Mr. Billings and the Lord, and that was that. This led to unplanned pregnancies, unmanageable families, a large surplus of children for export and an adoption industry. Nowadays, like motor car production, this is gone, relocated for a while in Romania, now in China. But on the other hand, if the information could be come by, abortion in England was also resorted to in desperation. Even though this latter practice was illegal in Ireland anyway, a group of energetic citizens of impeccable moral fibre sought to have a ban on abortion forever and ever amen inserted in the constitution just in case future generations might lose the run of themselves and let mere women decide. This caused 'The Referendum'[28] which changed nothing really—except legitimise everybody talking about and finding out the where, why and how much of abortion.

In the midst of all this, as a result of much agitation, and EEC Standards, the law on contraception had been eased so you could actually get a condom or whatever—but only from a doctor, and on prescription at that. Strongly implied in this was Sex=Disease, Contraception=Cure. Expensive business—if you planned a healthy sex-life it would have been cheaper to emigrate. The Well Woman Clinic was one of many family planning clinics which had previously got around the earlier law by giving out condoms free, in return for a small voluntary donation—they weren't

64

allowed to actually sell them (are you confused?). The people behind 'The Referendum' considered this outrageous and put pressure on religious elements within the State to prosecute the Well Women. So a Garda rookie was sent to the shebeen to purchase a condom which was to be 'Exhibit A' in a lawsuit. The song is the story, all true. A year or so later, after the things had been made legal and you could buy them in sweetie shops, the Clinic was finally fined £50 for their terrible crime.

***

The Johnnies Song

(Air: 'Johnny Jump Up')

In the year of nine-teen hundred and eighty-three
To save the un-born out we went, you and me
To canvass for votes in each church in the land
And we tould them if we lost, their souls would be damned.

In spite of them murderers we won the day,
Our courage and honesty was well repaid.
And the star of us all was a young Dublin cop;
To them evil Well-Women he dared put a stop.

From up in 'The Park' says the Guards' High Command:
"Them hussies will not flout the law in this land.
But since contraception revolts and disgusts
A strategy subtle apply here we must.

So we'll dress our top man in a jacket from Dunne's
And as a civilian he'll call to them ones."
That's how young Guard Johnny, unmarked, on a bike,
Came to call to The Well Woman Clinic one night,

As up Leeson Street this bould hero went ride- ing
To be undercover had him flushed with pride.
"Promotion will follow, no need to moon-light,"
Thought he at that shee-been as he alighted.

He took one last deep breath of oxygen sweet
Before he descended by stairs from the street,
Opened the door and himself he blessed
And thanked God that morning that he'd been to Mass—for

Set out in that place in full-colour relief
There was blatant contempt for religious belief:
The walls all around *in flagrante* displayed
Female components with details portrayed.

John's head spun round dizzy, his stomach was heave—ing
But sexual terror prevented him leave—ing.
A white-coated female then cut short his fright
Sayin', "For a customer here you've remarkable height!

Five-foot-eight,[29] I reckon, leads me to conclude
That you are a Guard and you possibly could
Be engaged in some stunt on behalf of the SPUC,[30]
You sneaky wee mouse, are you setting us up?"

Our john almost panicked but just managed to wink
And slip into the French-letter purchaser's slink.
She rolled up her eyes at this clever disguise,
Sayin': "You can't be careful with Vatican spies" – NOW!

Is it jelly you want, cream, or a sponge—or a cap?
A coil, or a letter—a tablet perhaps?"
(These terms muddled John, and caught him on the hop,
For they sounded like stuff from a wee huxter[31] shop.

He blushed and he asked her, "Can you please tell me
What is in that mountain of packets I see?"
She opened one up and says, "These here do be
Used for sex without babies or fear of disease."

She stretched it and blew it up like a balloon,
Let go and it flew like a bird round the room.
"Two pounds for ten and they come in maroon,
Yellow, blue, black, red, green, basket stitched and perfumed."

66

Poor Johnny felt sick and went weak at the knees;
Reviled in his eyes was manhood's dignity.
He paid for his evidence, him green in the face
And like a cat up the steps he escaped from that place.

But, next morning, recovered, returned that young Guard,
Only this time he showed them his Special Branch card.
"Ha-ha, me bould lassies, to the Bridewell we go,
For to sell me that thing was illegal, you know.

The cheek of yous women to take in your hands
The powers that the doctors alone must command.
Sex is disease, the law says in this land,
And them quare things are drugs and that's why they are banned.

Ireland's good name in the muck is bein' dragged
By self-righteous tramps who sell wee rubber bags
Designed for the kidnap and murder of sperm
Without as much mercy as Harpic [32] with germs."

In front of the High Court we wound up this tale
In defence of decrees made by celibate males;
To council the pregnant was treason we found
And the Well Woman clinic was fined fifty pound.

But alas, I conclude on a note of no hope
For although we believe in Ould Billings' and Pope's—words,
Our carpets are bulging with anguish and guilt—
For those feckers are still at it under the quilts.

© Fintan Vallely. This can be heard on the album
Big Guns and Hairy Drums

After a yarn told by singer Paul O'Brien at a 1997 Dick Gaughan Gig in Whelan's, re. a chat show interview he'd heard. In 1969 a few lads are supposed to have gone to the moon. Their names became household. One of them, Buzz Aldrin, is supposed to have given the thumbs up to the cameras up in space and uttered the words: "Good luck to you, Mr. Gorsky!" Since the period was bang in the middle of the Cold War, an intrigued CIA presumed that his words were a code to Russia, and in his debriefing they are supposed to have persecuted him. How and ever, he kept his lips sealed until after Mr. Gorsky died, and here is the story.

***

Good Luck to You, Mister Gorsky!

(Air: variation of 'I'll sing like a thrush on a hawthorn bush')

Buzz Aldrin, yes it's me, a household name you'll agree;
Good luck to you, Mister Gorsky!
I've chewed upon green cheese, I've supped tranquility;
Good luck to you, Mister Gorsky!
Perhaps you've wondered why I said those words on that great day
That I walked beneath the Milky Way, blowing Medieval thought away:
"Good luck to you, Mister Gorsky!"

Well, in nineteen-sixty-nine Richard Nixon'd walked the line;
Oh, Good luck to you, Mister Gorsky!
He rang us up and said, "Boys, I've found a way!"
Good luck to you, Mister Gorsky!
"Cold War heat is running high, power is in the sky,
Russian propaganda dogs are flying satellites:
"Good luck to you, Mister Gorsky!"

So myself and Neil were trained to cope with floating pens;
Good luck to you, Mister Gorsky!
Generously we were to find our act a step for all mankind
And so I said, "Good luck to you, Mister Gorsky!"
We gave the world our party pieces, and in the thirty second inter-stices
The CIA ironed out the creases, all the fucks and blinds and Jeezes
But not "Good luck to you, Mister Gorsky!"

Then we splashed down in the Pacific and, boys, it was terrific—
Good luck to you, Mister Gorsky!
Time-Life and television made a field day of our mission;
Good luck to you, Mister Gorsky!
But behind closed doors we were debriefed by faceless more-ons
Who scripted all our stor-ies, demanded could I tell them more:
'Why "Good luck to Mister Gorsky?"'

Well, they grilled me like a trout, direct and round about,
Why "Good luck to Mister Gorsky?"
I told them "Lads, I can't, in truth, know what I meant,
By 'Good luck to you, Mister Gorsky!'"
But I chanced, "Remember Jimmy Durante and his programme
     'sign-off' cant:
'Goodnight, Mrs Calabash, wherever you are.'*
So mine's: 'Good luck to you, Mister Gorsky'."

Well it's many years since then, me and me buddies are ould men;
Good luck to you, Mister Gorsky!
And poor Aldrin lost the game, in Boot Hill he's now lain;
Good luck to you, Mister Gorsky!
But now your wife and you've passed away, at last I'm free to have my say,
You'll recall my childhood days when I was your awful next-door neigh-
     bour,
"Good luck to you, Mister Gorsky."

*Comedian Jimmy Durante's customary sign-off at the end of his NBC television
show. Speculation continues as to whether Mrs Calabash was a real or fictional
person.

I put syrup on your chairs, rang your bell and ran away;
Good luck to you, Mister Gorsky!
I chased your cat and teased your dog, pinched apples, knocked your logs;
Good luck to you, Mister Gorsky!
But not once did you complain, instead directly you'd lay blame,
Puncture balls and bikes and fountain pens;
Good luck to you, Mister Gorsky!

So in this war one Sunday afternoon, I sneaked up beside your room;
Good luck to you, Mister Gorsky!
"Let's try oral sex!" you said to your wife there in the bed;
Good luck to you, Mister Gorsky!
Says she: "Get stuffed, you loon-ey! None of that you'll get me doin','"
Not till snow falls in mid-June, or that next-door brat walks on the moon!"
Good luck to you, Mister Gorsky!

If I'd told the CIA then, they'd have driven youse insane;
Good luck to you, Mister Gorsky!
Maybe deportation and the shame of house arrest and public blame;
So Good luck to you, Mister Gorsky!
But though the Berlin Wall's no longer there I've still no word of Mrs.
    Gorsky's prayer,
I'm embarrassed in despair—But, I'll ask of you up there
In the clouds,

Jesus!

How DID it go, Mister Gorsky?

© *Fintan Vallely*

Part 7: Cursory Comment

Putting a good curse on the wrongdoer is almost as good as a wrong being undone. Irish folklore is full of the stories. At the peak of the Famine evictions at Strokestown House in Roscommon, a woman put a curse on the place that a child would never be born therein. And the family indeed died out, and the house and lands eventually ended up in the hands of a descendant of a local peasant who officially opened it a couple of years ago with enough food and drink to choke and bloat the county, outrageously dedicating the lot to the issue of world famine. Curse songs set the sentiment of hatred to music, making them the direct opposite of a hymn. This version is No. 18 from Sam Henry's collection; it was said to be a symbolic reference to Robert Emmett.

***

Nell Flaherty's Drake

My name it is Nell, right candid I tell,
And I live near a hill, I ne'er will deny;
I had a large drake, the truth for to spake,
My grandfather left me when going to die.

71

He was merry and sound and would weigh twenty pound,
The universe 'round would I rove for his sake;
Bad luck to the robber, be he drunk or sober,
That murdered Nell Flaherty's beautiful drake.

His neck it was green and rare to be seen,
He was fit for a queen of the highest degree;
His body so white it would you delight,
He was fat, plump and heavy, and brisk as a bee.
This dear little fellow, his legs they were yellow,
He could fly like a swallow or swim like a hake.
But some wicked baggage to grease his white cabbage
Has murdered Nell Flaherty's beautiful drake.

May his pig never grunt, may his cat never hunt,
That a ghost may him haunt in the dark of the night.
May his hens never lay, may his horse never neigh,
May his goat fly away like an old paper kite.
May his duck never quack, may his goose be turned black
And pull down the stack with her long yella beak;
May the scurvy and itch never part from the britch
Of the wretch that has murdered Nell Flaherty's drake.

May his cock never crow, may his bellows ne'er blow,
Nor potatoes to grow—may he never have none;
May his cradle not rock, may his chest have no lock,
May his wife have no frock for to shade her backbone.
That the bugs and the fleas may this wicked wretch tease
And a piercing north breeze make him tremble and shake;
May a four-year-old bug build a nest in the lug
Of the monster who murdered Nell Flaherty's drake.

Make his pipe never smoke, may his teapot be broke
And to add to the joke may his kettle not boil;
May he be poorly fed till the hour he is dead,
May he always be fed upon lobsters and oil.
May he swell with the gout till his grinders fall out,
May he roar, howl and shout with a horrid toothache;
May his temple wear horns and his feet be all corns;
The wretch that has murdered Nell Flaherty's drake.

May his dog yelp and howl with hunger and could,
May his wife always scould till his brains go astray;
May the curse of each hag that e'er carried a bag
Light down on the wag till his head it turns grey.
May monkeys still bite him and mad dogs affright him
And everyone slight him asleep or awake;
May the rats ever gnaw him, and jackdaws still claw him,
The monster that murdered Nell Flaherty's drake.

But the only good news that I have to diffuse
Is of ould Peter Hughes and young Paddy McQuake,
And crooked Ned Manson, and big-nosed Bob Hanson,
Each one has a grandson of my beautiful drake.
Oh the bird he has dozens of nephews and cousins
And one I must have or my heart it will break
To keep my mind easy, or else I'll run crazy,
And so ends the song of my beautiful drake.

In January 1883, in the aftermath of what became known as "The Phoenix Park Murders" (6th May, 1882, the killing of Lord Frederick Cavendish and Thomas Henry Burke near Dublin) the police arrested twenty-seven men including the majority of the members of a secret group calling itself 'The Invincible Society'. One of them, James Carey, turned Queen's evidence and upon him the trial hinged. Six men were sentenced to death, four of them executed and the others were sentenced to penal servitude. James Carey, pre-empting the RUC's supergrass system, was freed, but on the way to Australia he was spotted and done in, giving rise to another song unconnected with this one. This is a gem among curse lyrics. It was written by James Fitzharris, a reputed songwriter of the times, nicknamed 'Skin the Goat', the cabman who drove the 'Invincibles' to and from the Phoenix Park. Charged with conspiracy, his divilmacare and stroppy court manner at the trial assisted the beak in giving him penal servitude for refusing to identify his passengers. Afterwards he himself became the hero of many songs on the subject of Carey. One of the stories about his nickname tells how he anticipated the bodhrán trade by about a hundred years and killed his treasured and much-loved goat to get a few bob for its skin. Seventeen years later he came back from exile to be fêted in song himself. He was further immortalised by James Joyce as the keeper of the 'Cabman's Shelter'.

***

Skin the Goat's Curse on Carey

Before I set sail I will not fail
To give that lad my blessing,
And if I had him here, there's not much fear
But he'd get a good top dressing;

By the hat on my head but he'd lie on his bed
Till the end of next September,
I'd give him good cause to rub his jaws
And Skin the Goat remember.

But as I won't get the chance to make Carey dance,
I'll give him my benedictions,
So from my heart's core may be evermore
Know nothing but afflictions.

May every buck flea from here to Bray
Jump through the bed that he lies on,
And by some mistake may he shortly take
A flowing pint of poison.

May his toes fill with corns like a puckawn's horns
Till he can neither wear slippers or shoes,
With a horrid toothache may he roar like a drake
And jump like a mad kangaroo.

May a horrid big rat make a hole in his hat
And chew all the hair off his head,
May the skin of a pig be made into a wig
And stuck on him when he is dead.

May the devil appear and fill him with fear,
And give him a kick of his club,
May hard paving stones and old horse's bones
Be all he can get for his grub.

May the sun never shine, nor the weather be fine
Whenever he walks abroad,
Till the day of his death may he have a bad breath
That will stink like a rotten old cod.

May his old wife be jealous and pitch up the bellows
Till the flames roar up over the head,
May he get such a fright he'll be turned left and right
Every night till it knocks him stone dead.

May a horrid baboon jump out of the moon
And tear his old carcass asunder,
And the day he'll set sail, may frost, snow and hail
Accompany rain and thunder.

That the world may know that Ireland's foe
Has left the shamrock shore,
And gone to stay at Hudson's Bay,
Or else in Baltimore.

When the equator is crossed, may the rudder be lost
And his vessel be wafted ashore,
To some cannibal isle near the banks of the Nile
Where savages jump and roar.

With a big sharp knife may they take his life
While his vessel is still afloat,
And pick his bones as clean as stones,
Is the prayer of poor Skin the Goat.

And if I die may my ghost sit on his bed-post
All the night till the morning-cock crow,
And you may surely swear, while I am there,
I'll squeeze him before I go.

*1883. Text from a broadside printed in Dublin,
now in the National Library of Ireland.*

The scattering described below by Finbar Boyle took place early on an Autumn morning in the year of 1985 in Oweny Callaghan's about-to-be-unlicensed premises in Crowe Street, Dundalk. In the company of about seventy others, Finbar was enjoying unparalleled hospitality and music; there was neither an insult traded nor a blow struck that anyone can remember and everyone would have eventually drifted home happily had they been let. Oweny afterwards left the pub trade and the town is miserable and quiet since.

***

The Night They Raided Oweny's

One evenin' of late down to Crowe Street I strayed
To a bar that is famous for doin' a late trade
In vodka, beer, whiskey and red lemonade
Among company that's kindly and cordial.
The man from Kinawley put me at my ease
And he sat me down cosy before a great blaze
And he filled me a pint and a half-un that pleased
All freshly come over the Border.

For an hour and a half I drank liquor so rare
You would think it was brewed by the gods I declare
Out of nectar and honey and lotuses fair
All just only over the border.
Then at half-past eleven I sadly prepared
To return to my lodging back where I was reared;
I packed up my bags, I was filled with dull care,
And then Oweny put in a big order.

So the tipplers relaxed and returned to their drinks
Rejoicing that now they need not feel the pinch.
Peter Short finished off the last eighth of an inch
He was suckin' since twenty past seven.

And the music began in the old-fashioned style,
You would travel to hear it for many the mile.
I was drinkin' and laughin' away all the while;
I thought I was dead and in heaven.

There were lads there from Newry, from 'Rock and The Hack,
Some that came from Belfast that never went back,
And more lived convenient to Carrolls and Blacks
And every manjack swillin' porter.
There were some came from Hill Street and more from the Quay,
Some Crossmaglen patriots tearin' away;
Inniskeen, Donaghmoyne, they were all in array,
But each man kept himself in good order.

Now a dirty big Guard that was out on the street
On passing the door heard the music so sweet
And he kicked up his heels and he beat a retreat
To summon up two of his cronies.
They quickly returned to the scene of the crime
And they called on the company to fight or resign.
"Let them in," cried Pat Murphy, "We'll only be fined,"
On the night that the Guards raided Oweny's

Says the sergeant on entering, "What's this I see,
And why are so many out on the spree?
Can it be that the country at long last is free?
Your conduct it is most nefarious."
"Sergeant, it's not free," then Oweny did say,
"If you wish to drink beer like the rest you must pay.
We'll stay here if we like till the clear light of day—
Sure you know in Dundalk we're gregarious."

Then the Guards went around and they took all our names;
They struggled to spell with their feeble wee brains'
And of some names in Irish they made a great hames
And more they abandoned forever.
To the roof the Mulhollands some quickly did climb
To gaze from afar on the scene of the crime
And to watch the ould Guards makin' good overtime
As they gathered the lads altogether.

May the divil he roast them high up on a ramp,
The Sergeant, the Guard and the lad with the lamp,
The dirty mean miserable, lousy low tramps
From the bog that were dragged up so lowly;
May they always see suffering, sorrow and pain,
May their boots never fit, may their belts never strain,
If they interrupt such a grand evenin' again
As the night that they first raided Oweny.

That their motors may stand, that their noses may run,
That their necks now so red may turn green in the sun,
That their teeth may turn black and fall out one by one,
That starvation may make them grow bony;
That their arses may fester and drop to their heels,
That their last dying minutes may be tempered with squeals,
That they may dance for ever the fastest of reels
With the Divil for raiding poor Oweny.

© *Finbar Boyle*

The poet Patrick O'Kelly, a native of Galway, was a wildly-attired, persuasive and honey-tongued devil in his day. For a living he wrote, sang and traded in broadside ballads, eventually managing to inveigle himself into the company of King George IV through flogging him fifty songbooks and refusing the proffered £50, preferring instead to have an audience with the Big Lad up in the Phoenix Park. The monarch was so impressed that he spoke nicely to O'Kelly and presented him with a gold watch. The poet traded far and wide on this reputation, so much so that he scundered his public. Sick of all this, some of them robbed him of the bauble in the town of Doneraile, Co. Cork, but regretted it when revenge was returned on them in the form of a song cursing the town. This was printed in a book in 1808, one story having it that it had no effect, another holding that it caused such notorious insult to the village's honesty that the traders, through Lady Doneraile, persuaded O'Kelly to withdraw the affront in exchange for another timepiece. Like *The Peeler and the Goat*, though, the song was so good it had already travelled beyond recall or redemption, but the poet got the watch, his dignity back, revenge, and he was supposedly even more insufferable from then on.

[Information from *Popular Songs of Ireland,* by T. Crofton Croker.]

***

The Doneraile Litany

Alas! How dismal is my tale!
I lost my watch in Doneraile,
My Dublin watch, my chain and seal,
Pilfered at once in Doneraile.

May fire and brimstone never fail
To fall in showers on Doneraile,
May all the leading fiends assail
The thieving town of Doneraile.

As lightnings flash across the vale
So down to hell with Doneraile,
The fate of Pompey at Pharsale
Be that the curse of Doneraile.

May beef or mutton, lamb or veal
Be never found in Doneraile
But garlic soup and scurvy kail
Be still the food for Doneraile.

And moving forward as the creeping snail
Th'industry be of Doneraile,
May heaven a chosen curse entail
On rigid, rotten Doneraile.

May sun and moon for ever fail
To beam their lights in Doneraile,
May every pestilential gale
Blast that cursed spot called Doneraile.

May no sweet cuckoo, thrush or quail
Be ever heard in Doneraile,
May patriot kings and commonweal
Despise and harass Doneraile.

May every great Post, Gazette and Mail,
Sad tidings bring of Doneraile,
May loudest thunders ring a peal
To blind and deafen Doneraile.

May vengeance fall at head and tail
From north to south at Doneraile,
May profit light and tardy sale
Still damp the trade of Doneraile.

May Fame resound a dismal tale
Whene'er she lights on Doneraile,
May Egypt's plagues at once prevail
To thin the knaves of Doneraile.

May frost and snow and sleet and hail
Benumb each joint in Doneraile,
May wolves and bloodhounds trace and trail
The cursed crew of Doneraile.

May Oscar, with his fiery flail,
To atoms thresh all Doneraile,
May every mischief, fresh and stale,
Abide, henceforth, in Doneraile.

May all, from Belfast to Kinsale
Scold, curse and damn you, Doneraile,
May neither floor nor oaten meal
Be found or known in Doneraile.

May want and woe each joy curtail
That e'er was known in Doneraile,
May no one coffin want a nail
That wraps a rogue in Doneraile.

May all the thieves that rob and steal
The gallows meet in Doneraile,
May all the sons of Granaweal
Blush at the thieves of Doneraile.

May mischief, fig as Norway whale,
O'erwhelm the knaves of Doneraile,
May curses, wholesale and retail
Pour with full force on Doneraile.

May every transport wont to sail
A convict bring from Doneraile,
May every churn and milking pail
Fall dry to staves in Doneraile.

May cold and hunger still congeal
The stagnant blood of Doneraile,
May every hour new woes reveal
That hell reserves for Doneraile.

May every chosen ill prevail
O'er all the imps of Doneraile,
May no-one wish or prayer avail
To soothe the woes of Doneraile.

May th' Inquisition straight impale
The raparees of Doneraile,
May Charon's boat triumphant sail
Completely manned for Doneraile.

Oh! may couplets never fail
To find a curse for Doneraile,
And may grim Pluto's inner gaol
For ever groan with Doneraile.

In December 1996 a neighbour's small girl was given a kitten. After a week of it shiting all over her family's place and causing terror and marital stress the beast was carefully and anonymously placed outside our obviously friendly home where it pawed the window resourcefully for two and a half days in the dead of winter before we cracked and took it in. A cat costs the same to run for a year as the central heating in a small house (presuming one gets a summer), and so, as this friendly item displayed the miracle of progressive cell-multiplication, it burrowed its way into our pockets as well as out hearts. A cat-door had to be installed to eliminate the whining harangue that only a cat can pull off successfully (and then get comforted for); people had to be programmed to be there when the natives weren't about to pour out its mad-cow mush, soybean nuggets and water = a cat is bother too. And next thing, in due course the neighbouring scraggy, battle-scarred, mange-ridden, mongrel male, wall-top survivors began to develop another level of interest in it. So it had to be neutered. This cost the same as a meal for two (with wine), but still cheaper than a flock of kittens, and demanded our son experiencing a Blue Cross queue of shaven-head hard lads with spike-collared Dobermans and into-the-west piebald ponies. All were levelled by common cause: they huddled around each beast in earnest discussion of pregnancy prevention, 'flu, colic and sore paws and hooves.

For a week or two the cat's bald-patch and frightening potato-sack, bag-stitched scar was the wonder of the neighbouring small girls, but we survived that, even if the garden didn't. At last the hair was growing, a new hormonal regime took over and great affection was enjoyed by all; until one fine day, in a blink, while sitting on the window-sill, the street busy—it disappeared and was never seen again. This is what happens to cats (when they are not run over). A kitten is for Christmas, a cat comes out of considerable patience and faith, a loved cat is a friendly cat, and nothing knows better how to return attention. Some bastard stole it. The small girls never once called to the door after that. Mysteriously.

Poet Michael Hartnett of Newcastle West, Co. Limerick had a similar experience and minced no words about his feelings.

***

On Those Who Stole Our Cat, A Curse

On those who stole our cat, a curse:
may they always have an empty purse
and need a doctor and a nurse
    prematurely;
may their next car be a big black hearse
    oh may it, surely.

May all their kids come down with mange,
their eldest daughter start acting strange,
and the wife start riding the range
    (and I don't mean the Aga);
when she begins to go through the change
    may she go gaga.

And may the husband lose his job
and have great trouble with his knob
and the son turn out a yob
    and smash the place up;
may he give his da a belt in the gob
    and mess his face up!

And may the granny end up in jail
for opening her neighbours' mail,
may all that clan moan weep and wail,
    turn grey and wizened
on the day she doesn't get bail
    but Mountjoy prison!

Oh may their daughter get up the pole,
and their drunken uncle lose his dole,
for our poor cat one day they stole
    may they rue it!
And if there is a black hell-hole
    may they go through it!

Unfriendly loan-sharks to their door
as they beg for one week more;
may the seven curses of Inchicore
    rot and blight 'em!
may all their enemies settle the score
    and kick the shite of 'em!

I wish rabies on all their pets,
I wish them a flock of bastard gets,
I wish 'em a load of unpayable debts,
    TV Inspectors—
to show them a poet never forgets
    his malefactors.

May rats and mice them ever hound
may half of them be of mind unsound,
may their house burn down to the ground
    and no insurance;
may drugs and thugs their lives surround
    beyond endurance!

May God forgive the heartless thief
who caused our household so much grief;
if you think I'm harsh, sigh with relief
I haven't even started.
I can do worse. I am, in brief,
    yours truly, Michael Hartnett.

October, 1994

*from A Book of Strays (2002) by kind permission of The Gallery Press
and the Estate of Michael Hartnett*

Part 8: Drink, Drugs And Debauchery

Ditties against drink were common in the ancient Temperate times of the 2nd—6th decades of the century of Technology. Typical is the following :

> It was the pig-fair last September, a day I will remember,
> I was marching up and down in drunken pride
> When my knees began to flutter, I lay down in the gutter
> And a pig came up, and stretched out by my side.
> As I lay there with a stutter, thinking thoughts I could not utter
> I thought I heard a passing lady say
> "You can tell the one who boozes, by the company that he chooses"
> And at that, the pig got up, and walked away.

From time to time you read in the papers of pigs being fed on stale beer, and both liking it and thriving on it. No one ever considers the health-giving properties of alcoholic substances among the human species, though. The papers are full of dark warnings on health damage and all the rest. So important was the crusade against drink that no stone was left unturned in the efforts to stamp it out: even in the dark days of the Great Famine, Temperance crusading was at its height. Midst epidemic and disastrous blight back in Ireland, neighbours turned their backs on each other once cholera struck, and even the then Catholic Primate in Armagh—William Crolly—died of it. Father Matthew, our fervent Temperance crusader, ran away from it and abandoned the flock at home in July, 1849 supposedly to seek the lost sheep in America, there comforting the fears, faith and thankfulness of the survivors of the coffin ships by lathering them with guilt. Inside two years he had doled out half a million 'pledges' agin drink.

'The pledge', with it's holier than thou 'Pioneer pin' was a kind of Ku Klux Klan against drink, and acted as a safety valve. But it is a thing of the past really now, having been replaced by the much more sensible AA, where it's not up to God, but yourself. It has also been totally undermined by children drinking, and also by *Dallas*—where nobody ever appeared unless there was a drink in their hand, the *druth* thus created driving the watchers out to the pub in droves after the show ended each night; if you watched it on two channels you were in trouble. 'The pin' image has also been severely damaged by lads who used it as a "leave me alone" flag of convenience when they ran out of money or were saving up for a spree, were in danger of dying, or when they had been threatened with being left by an unfortunate, distracted wife. A good plea in court on behalf of the defendant used to be, "he's taken the pledge your honour" (if the other standard, "he's signed up to join the Army, your honour" didn't work). The pledge wasn't important for women since they didn't have money, and, even where they did, they were unlikely to be so gullible as to listen to advice from a man in a long dress who lashed back a couple of glasses of wine first thing every morning. And so there are many songs about drinking.

But the songs in favour of drink are much better, even if they do preserve stereotypes. This one is from the Temperance period—even while Father Matthew was fighting starvation by demanding drought, wicked scribes were chuckling and drooling with ecstasy at the fine lines they could pen as guerrilla warfare against his legions. This song by an unidentified tippler—just the sort of person every publican needs more of—appears in *Songs and Ballads of Ireland*, published in 1901.

***

Paddy's Panacea

Let your quacks in newspapers be cutting their capers
'Bout curin' the vapours, the scurvy or gout

88

With their powders and potions, their balsams and lotions,
Ochone! In their notions they're mightily out.
Would you know the true physic to bother the phthssic
And pitch to the divil cramp colic and spleen?
You'll find it, I think, if you take a big drink
With your mouth to the brink of a jug of poteen.
    Then stick to the craytur, the best thing in nature,
    For sinkin' your sorrows and raising your joys.
    Oh whack botheration! No dose in the nation
    Can give consolation like whiskey me boys.

Oh, no liquid cosmetic for lovers athletic
Or ladies pathetic can give such a bloom,
And for sweets, by the powers—a whole garden of flowers
Never gave their own bowers such a darlin' perfume.
Then the liquor so rare, if you're willin' to share,
To be turnin' your hair when it's grizzled or red;
Sure the sod has the merit to make the true spirit
So strong it'll turn both your hair and your head.
    Then stick to the craytur, the best thing in nature
    For sinkin' your sorrows and raisin your joys;
    Oh! Since it's perfection, no doctor's direction
    Can guard the complexion like whiskey me boys.

Whilst a child in the cradle, my nurse with a ladle
Was filling her mouth with a notion of pep
When a drop from the bottle slipped into me throttle,
I capered and wriggled right out of her lap.
On the floor I lay sprawling, and roaring and bawling,
Till father and mother were both to the fore,
All sobbing and sighing they conceived I was dying
But soon found I only was crying for more.
    Then stick to the craytur, the best thing in nature
    For sinkin' your sorrows and raisin' your joys;
    Oh! What! How they'd chuckle, if babes in their truckle
    They could only suckle with whiskey me boys.

Through my youthful progression, through years of discretion,
My childhood's impression still clung to me mind,
For at school and college, the bolus of knowledge
I never could grip till with whiskey combined.

And as older I'm growin', time's ever bestowin'
On Erin's potato a flavour so fine, that
Howev'r they may lecture 'bout Job and his nectar
Itself is the only true liquid divine.
    Then stick to the craytur, the best thing in nature
    For sinkin' your sorrows and raisin' your joys;
    Oh! Whack 'tis delightin', for courtin' or fightin'
    There's nought so excitin' as whiskey me boys.

Let Philosophers dabble in science and babble
'Bout oxygin, hydrogin, nitrogin's fame—
For their gin to my thinkin' is not worth the drinkin',
Their labour's all lost and their larnin' a dream.
They may prate by the score of their elements four
That all things earth, air, fire and water must be;
For their rules I don't care, for in Ireland I'll swear
By St. Pat there's a fifth—and that's whiskey Machree!
    Then stick to the craytur, the best thing in nature
    For sinkin' your sorrows and raisin' your joys.
    Och! Whack art and science! Myself bids defiance
    To yield in appliance to whiskey me boys.

Come guess me this riddle—what beats pipes and fiddle?
What's stronger than mustard and milder than cream?
What best wets your whistle, what's clearer than crystal
And sweeter than honey and stronger than steam?
What'll make the dumb talk, what'll make the lame walk?
What's the elixir of life and philosopher's stone?
And what helped Mr. Brunnel to dig the Thames tunnel—
Sure wasn't it the spirit of neat Innisowen?
    Then stick to the craytur, the best thing in nature
    For sinkin' your sorrows and raisin' your joys;
    Oh Whack, I'd not wonder, if lightnin' and thunder
    Was made from the plunder of whiskey me boys.

*Anon, from the singing of Tim Lyons, verse 5 courtesy of Jane Flynn,
Miltown Malbay. This song can be heard on Tom Munnelly's collection of
Tom Lenihan's songs, The Mount Callan Garland.*

The EC elections are celebrated by utter boredom by the voters all over the continent—a mere forty-something % turnout in Ireland in 1994 says this most eloquently. For it seems to the plain people that this is about voting for a well paid job for someone who already has a well-paid job, and the only people seriously interested are political parties and the media. For all of them this is the industry which produces most of their wages and fun. While the entry of Ireland to the EC since 1972 has produced an unprecedented upping of living standards and improvement in social legislation, a dismantling of the political power of the Catholic Church and a refreshing undermining of mythology in political life, the down side has been the disappearance of local industry, dashed hopes, false promises, automated pubs, being humiliated by machines embedded in walls, malls full of boring chain shops in Dublin and other awfulness. Tim Lyons is a sceptic and is particularly concerned about drink—the assault on the price of it and the pretentiousness of some of its suppliers as they vie to outdo each other with tacky names taken off the TV. And yes, 'Miss Ellie's' does exist, and no, there's no 'Grotto Bar' in Knock (but there is a 'Grotto' burger joint). 'Porter' refers to Guinness, the term originating in the cheap ale brewed for porters in London markets in the 19th century.

***

The E(?)C Song

Will yis give me some order a minute
Till I sing yis a verse of a song;
Will yis please hould yer whisht for a second
Or I'll pitch the whole bloody thing wrong.
It's concerning the state of the country
Since we joined with the community,
And partic'l'rly the price of the porter
And all products marked double E C.

I'm an aisy-goin' kind of a fella
(Too aisy some might remark)
But there's times when the kittle boils over
And the quietest of dogs has to bark.
I flew over from London last Friday,
I came home for the *ceol* and the crack,
But my sterling devalued so swiftly
I'm having for to take the boat back.

Now it's not that I want things all perfect;
It's just that I want to survive.
But it now seems that we weren't doin' too badly
Before we aligned with 'The Five'.
It's fourteen long years since we joined them,
(I remember the Thursday quite well);
The pint was roughly three shillings
Poised on the mad brink of hell.

And if you think that it's bad down the country
You should see what they're paying in 'The Pale'.
The print on their price-lists is tiny
To protect those not hearty and hale.
And a sandwich is out of the question
You'll have to eat crisps or ould nuts,
For the cost of the wheat is ferocious
And it's fixed by those Belgian scuts.

We expected cheap whiskey from Scotland,
Cheap wine from the depths of the lake,
Thick slices of beef off the mountain,
Olive oil, goose paté and cake,
Cheap Château Margaux from the Bordeaux,
Cases of gold Avocaat;
All we got was free love from Stockholm—
And you all know the price paid for that.

Have you seen the quare names on our pubs now?
They're called after actors and shows:
Now it's 'Magnum's' and 'Dillingers' and 'Southfork'
Where it used to be 'Murphy's' or 'Keogh's'.
They're opening one up now in Feakle
And calling it 'Mountain Street Blues'.
But they've got it all wrong down in Kerry
There's one there called 'The Nine O'Clock News'.

I walked into a place in the market
But couldn't get served at the bar.
Says the barmaid, "Sit down at a table
And give me a ring for a jar."
So I set meself down in the corner
And dialled bar extension 0-2,
But bad cess to Bord Telecom Éireann—
I could see her but I couldn't get through.

So farewell to ould Ireland forever,
I've had it right up to my neck
Fond mem'ries of good times surround me
As I'm standing alone on the deck.
It's taking me back over to England
On the waves of my own Irish Sea;
A curse on you, Brussels and Europe,
And bad luck to your double E C.

© Tim Lyons. This song can be heard on the album Big Guns and Hairy Drums

"Once upon a time there was, Irish ways and Irish laws." So the song sung by, among others, Christy Moore and then Sinéad O'Connor, goes. The most rudimentary history books tell us that in old Ireland the Gaelic way of life was opposed in every way to 'English' ideas of civilisation. This condition does not exist exclusively in the past, for the issue is not so much about what is done, but how it is done. So too with the business of constant need for drink to lighten the burden of living in a 'cool temperate' (freezing damp depressing) climate. In the olden days people got around it by making their own poteen. But with the invention of Revenue this became a crime, so the stills moved to the hills and swamps until such time as the Bunsen burner, bottled gas, the indirect immersion cylinder and sugar were invented—whereupon the industry moved back to the kitchen. However, people in general seem to be so tuned to job-oriented society that they are happy enough to use the pub rather than make it themselves. But since it is vital that all drink-related laws simply must be broken (as a matter of historically-ordained principle), consumption has now replaced production as the area of legal contest. Drink-driving produces a large, healthy revenue for the Gardaí, insurance brokers and taxi companies, and of course the Medical profession (among whom there would be huge job losses were we not so self-destructive). At the safer end of this spectrum the laws used to be not so much challenged as bent a bit: most pub customers were thrown out at 'Time!'—but a chosen few, well vetted for discretion (and, cynically, although they may not have been aware of it, particularly for solvency) were sometimes let stay. All very sociable, fulfilling the needs of both the late-oriented who exist in every society, and the bank balance of the publican. Moral pressures eventually came to bear on this arrangement however, as the age of the average drinker has tumbled to about twelve with the invention of the Lounge Bar and the Confirmation-pay awards. So eventually under the guise of benefiting the tourist industry, drinking-up time was extended a bit (tourists from the next street were the main beneficiaries— when did you ever see a real tourist with anything other than a stale half-glass at closing time?).

But this was all too late to prevent the invention of the notorious night club. 'Night Club' conjures up images of Paris after dark, with dickie-bowed, tailed males draped casually on wickerwork chairs being engaged in refined, artistic discussion with ball-clad, sinuous women inhaling smouldering leafy gases via long cigarette holders. This was not the case in Ireland. Wherever we go we seem likely to recreate the cramped conditions of the average 1950s, large-family living space. Hence the pubs for long were tiny (for all the demand for them), and indeed unless you can't move then the place is no good. 'Night clubs' in the 1980s and 1990s were even tinier, usually being located in Georgian coal cellars in Dublin's grander areas. The rooms were as dark as possible, walls were often covered in mirrors to hide the damp and create the illusion of being in a much bigger coal cellar that stretched to infinity; lighting was a couple of sets of traffic lights which presumably were still considered a novelty by the largely ex-rural clientele. There was a DJ who played selected discs (selected for moronic beat) with the volume amplified to about a million watts. Nobody went there to talk. Many went to dance, but the main reason the clubs were there was to sell or consume drink after hours. There was a sexual thing too—you went there to get off your mark, or not. Every sex-craving suited male in the city seemed to be present, often complete with red tie and baby-blue pullover washed by the wife at home. And the odd wife not at home there too. Often politicians adorned these spots, and that's why they existed, the territory being—for affairs and cavortions—considered a sort of no person's land, an Emperor's new clothes of divarsion. Since the owner's only objective was profit, the drink was a ferocious price, and cheap, cheap plonk was sold for the same price per bottle as you would pay for a full tank of petrol. Usually when people got there—they operated from 12 until 5am or so—they were too drunk to notice the price—or to drink the wine—and more often than not they stole each other's anyway, but nobody cared as they smiled benignly at each other (you couldn't be heard).

Michael Marrinan obviously slipped out to such an institution one night—only to find, as often happens, that his spouse had the same ideas about alleviation of marital boredom, and was flying it on the edge as well. If they hadn't caught each other out we would never have had this song.

***

The Night-Clubbing Song

(Air: 'Larry O'Gaff', 'Tatter Jack Walsh')

Well I'll sing of the capers of the rockers and shakers
That are out all the night 'til the break of the day;
Some just of the cradle and more hardly able,
In every night club sure they boogie away.
Some they are arguing and some are blaguarding
And more in these clubs they are quite indisceet;
Where the lights they are flashing and the music 'tis crashing,
In this latest fashion of imported beat.

Well these clubs I am stating will sure take some bating
With no band at all but a music machine,
Your man stands at the table without spoon or ladle
And pours out his goods on the boogeying scene.
And it's not surprising when the music starts rising
To see him put a muffler on each of his ears,
While those that are dancing and maybe romancing
Are losing their hearing forever I fear.

Well if you must ask me or maybe attack me
For finding meself in this place so designed,
Well the wife was away for the night she did say,
"With the oul' ICA" for to knit was confined.
Ah but out in the morning without any warning
Out there on the dance floor I was tasting new life;
On the floor with a hippie there sliding and slipping
Was the shape and the make of me own darling wife.

Well in due recognition she winked in a fashion,
The eyelid on my side being all that was free.
'Twas no use us talking with the music there squawking,
'Twas then that l wished I was at a céilí.
Then an ould lad before me had words so adoring
To say to his partner he couldn't hold out,
So instead of a whisper in her ear this ould jester
Delivered his message be way of her mouth.

96

There was some oscillating and some contemplating
And some they were ating what I couldn't see,
And some were still learning and I was discerning
If any young wan had an eye out for me.
Balloons from the ceiling were soon disappearing,
One young lad was searching for more on the floor,
When a boy with elation gave three cheers for the nation
Whose letters have lately reached this our fair shore.

The shapes they were makin' if I'm not mistaken
Will leave their legs achin' for more than a year,
With their jivin and boppin' and leppin' and hoppin'
And never a trace of a jig or a reel.
If I was in Burma or maybe Uganda
Or deep in the southern Argentine
Those dancing gyrations that they're perpetrating
I'd not be debating in their native scene.

I love all set-dances, the polka,s the lancers,
In Kerry the slides, up in Clare jigs and reels,
And what's seldom seen now like a horse with a plough,
Well what I wouldn't give for a few double wheels.
But now they are training and daily explaining
The old ways of dancing to young girls and boys,
So the discos they'll be leavin' to be misbehavin'
At sessions and céilis forever me boys.

This song can be heard on Mícheál Marrinan's album Between Miltown &
Ennistymon. Information and his other lyrics are on http://www.irishsongs.net/.

(Schitheredee version of this song appears in the Appendix, p. 238).

'DS (detectives) Wright and DS Spencer responded to a possible suicide attempt by jumping off the 17th floor of the Grand Cypress (hotel). While they tackled the subject, Detective Ford was gathering intelligence information from Dunne's room. During that process an approximate 31.5 grammes of cocaine was located in Dunne's luggage with his ID. Def (defendant) was finally subdued and was found to have additional cocaine in his possession. Def was transported to Sand Lake hospital then CBOd. Def is a resident of Ireland. The money in his room was taken into evidence for safe keeping ($9,738). Capt La Forte and Major Marcus on the scene.'
—Police Report on Ben Dunne's Arrest

"DUNNES STORES BETTER VALUE BEATS THEM ALL" used be the famous slogan of Ireland's most competitive cut-price supermarket which specialises in selling the fastest-moving items at the lowest prices. It's exactly what a country, with two thirds of its population dependent, needs, and young Ben Dunne knew it. Nerve in the business field however earned him no sympathy when he finally fell off the wall: on an alleged golfing trip to Miami he OD'd on cocaine and went off his rocker. The primary schools were full of the jokes within the week and young Ben was the laughing stock of the underdogs, while po-faced articles by business colleagues in the national press tried to rescue his image and put it all down to him being under terrible stress (as if cocaine wasn't the richer person's hit, and businessmen with money didn't hire sexual partners). This was on our screens and in our press for two weeks. Dunne pleaded guilty. Later on in the year, with his trial over and him got off, he appeased the Knights of Columbanus by joining in the Irish supermarket blockade against selling condoms: "Our customers wouldn't like it", "There's no demand", etc etc.[33]

***

98

Dunne(s) Stor(i)es Beats Them All

(Air: 'Dunn Song', 'Green Grow the Rushes', 'Red fly the Banners', etc, or else the plain, simple tune 'Dingle Regatta' —third part)

I'll sing you a story that starts with keeping people fed
Mincemeat, fish fingers, sugar, tay, jam, beans and cut-price bread.
Ben Dunne had shops in Dublin, Bangor, Armagh, Cork and Derr-
-Y, Trading under this proud pledge:
DUNNE'S STORES BETTER VALUE BEATS THEM ALL.

Well, there were big Dunne's, and wee Dunne's
And lots of Shopping Centre Dunne's,
The scourge of Quinn's and Quinnsworth Dunne's,
Dunne's Stores beat them all.
And when oul St. Bernard's race was run
His place was took by younger Dunne,
The market-leaders' rising son, Dunne Stores STILL beat them all.

Now this young Dunne was a thorough bloke,
To get new supplies he'd go for broke
To lose opponents in the smoke,
For Dunne's Stores had to beat them all.
So in search of a market master stroke—
He'd heard about Miami's tokes—
With a new line in St. Bernard Coke
Dunne's Stores would beat them al.

Well, then, there was high Dunne and low Dunne,
Under Dunne and over Dunne,
In the bed and in the bathtub done,
Dunne's story beat them all.
Front-page in the Monday *Sun,*
His golfing secrets were undone
When all was tould by some young one,
Dunne's story beat them all.

In defence Ben said that making bread
Had stressed him out and turned his head
And left him very easy led;
Dunne's story beat them all.
Thon dark-haired lassie was misled
To think he'd paid for getting laid—
He'd sooner shop in Quinnsworth instead;
Dunne's story beat them all.

And while others done for drugs are shunned,
End up in jail or on the run,
Miami Vice sent home Ben Dunne,
His story beat them all.
At commercial travellers' high-rise fun
Young Saint Bernard's number one—
But they won't sell condoms in Ben Dunne's
For Dunne Stores beats them all.

Then on came Bacchanalian
Rhymesters and comedians,
They raised their glasses to young Dunne,
For his story beat them all.
There were endless hours of ruthless fun,
From slagging jokes to bad taste puns,
And before the court case had even begun
Dunne stories beat them all.

Jumpers on the seventeenth floor,
Underpants beside the door,
Free draw for Escorts with each Coke;
"Dunne's scores beats them all."
Trolley-pushers banned in Ben Dunne shops,
Deals on wheels is for the chop,
Piped music's gone, the crack's been stopped;
Dunne stories beat them all.

Once the stone was turned
Out crawled the worms—
Lowry, gifts, and Tax returns,
Albert brought the house down too—

Dunne's stores shopped them all.
The moral of this tale's not pure—
Connected men can open doeurs
One law for rich, and one for poor—
Dunne's story beats them all.

So let all ye part-time checkout staff
And even spotty blue-suits laugh,
For this yarn's true, and Ben Dunne rue-s
That his-story beat them all.
For-if he-had yous on full time way-
-Ges and paid you for your holidays,
He wouldn't be this way today
And his-story beat them all.

And pay me heed ye business breed
In Jaguars and Merceed-es,
Who'd squeeze the last threeha'pence from
The many hands that feeds yis.
You say that Unions[34] stand for greed—
But look at what yis do with what yous don't even need,
So stuff your starchy handkerchiefs,
Dunne's story beats yis all.

CHORUS:
Die, didd-ley-eye, diddely die,
Dee, die-dlee-eye, die-dlee-eye, die-dlee-eye, di,
Die, didd-ley-eye, diddely die
Dee Die-diddley die-diddley
Da, Roh.

© *Fintan Vallely. This song can be heard on the album Big Guns and Hairy Drums.*

Part 9: Gulpinism [35]

I n Ireland the memory of the Great Famine persists to this day. It does not matter if there are or were other famines in the world, naturally the one we are perpetually concerned about is our very own which still lives on in the minds of very old people who were told about it by other very old people who were told about it by their parents who lived through it. Consequently the issue of food is a serious one. The average child gets murdered, killed or destroyed at least a hundred times before the age of eighteen for not coming home in time for the dinner. As a result, by the time young people are of pub-going age, they are conditioned to eating at regular intervals.

Aware that the historical deficiency in potatoes is, in fact, a genetic condition and constitutes a 'black hole' in our psyche, entrepreneurs have moved swiftly to organise—on every street corner, in every back alley, at every wind- and rain-swept tourist attraction behind every whin bush, at every dogfight, even in Dublin's sumptuous Grafton Street for the wealthy migrant, in the heart of New York, Boston and London for the lonely exile, for the Irish traveller abroad in Hong Kong, Sydney, Düsseldorf, Berlin, Vienna, Zurich and now even Moscow—to organise some means of supplying, at any hour of the day or night, a potato-starved people with the food their great-grandmothers and great-grandfathers died for the want of. And so, once the pub customers are evicted each night, all troop out to either the chipper—the 'Chuck wagon', 'Frying Irishman', or 'Golden Spoon' (it may be a building, a lorry, a van or just a car trailer) or to the Chinese version—'Rice Paddy', 'Chow Mine', 'Rosary Star', etc—for chips. No day is completed without potatoes. The social life at the chip shop was second only to Sunday mass, and now only to Sunday morning at the recycling, and is certainly the most recent thing most 'lads' can recall on a Sunday morning, especially if the produce has been recycled instantly as dog food (dogs enjoy the musty hop flavour).

Tim Lyons personally has no time at all for chips and burgers (except when absolutely necessary) and for several years now has been of the opinion that the Fast Food industry is fattening the entire Western Hemisphere beyond its needs and will eventually kill it off. This theory was developed over the Willie Clancy week in Miltown Malbay in West Clare in 1987. After a hearty nights singing and socialising, Tim emerged at four in the morning from a certain pub to find that the street was like a scene from *The Brothers Karamazov* with chip vans and their generators roaring and belching black smoke, fire-eaters gushing volcanic evocations, wild, feckless flute, fiddle and bodhrán reels, native concertina and primitive Paolo-Soprani, the crystal-shattering contests of once-athletic youth and the wild, skrawking ca-hoos of comely maidens broken out from the bondage of their firesides—all a reckless reconstruction of the passion of The Creation, of Baghdad and the cradle of civilisation, of the Tuatha De Danann and their exodus from Morocco—of Bob Quinn and Frankie Gavin—of a direct line back through the aeons, throbbing in the balmy July night air. Even John Taylor[36] in far-off Strangford heard about it and was so horrified that he entirely reconstructed protestant identity to avoid his flock hearing about it and wanting to join in.

But particularly nostalgic was the tantalising smell of roasting flesh, itself reminiscent of the feasting of our own Red Branch Knights[37] at Eamhain Macha, lifetimes before Jesus or mad cows were ever heard of. All this coalesced in a heady spirit of divilmecaredness and Neanderthal bliss, causing Tim to dip into his pocket and purchase a charcoal burger from a contraption made of an old gate and chicken wire set up on two tar barrels and fired by bits of polystyrene. He should have known. While evolution continued to reverse itself in town, Tim spent the next three days in a tent lashed by the gales on the White Strand (and most of that was on the toilet) doubled up in excruciating agony as his body battled with the dark forces of anaerobia and microbiology. He commemorates the event here and warns of the impending doom and destruction of the Nation, describing how unsavoury and uncouth we are once the hunger bites. No mercy is given to either consumers or suppliers, and the lambasting ends with an exhortation to us all to (re?) turn to the wholesome health-farm fare (whose only purpose is to encourage healthier emissions from that very part of the body), fare that none of us—least of all Tim—would even dream of eating.

***

The Fast-Food Song

There is today around this land, a most unhealthy fad,
Inspired by neighbour Uncle Sam, promoting all that's bad;
With eating soggy burger buns, and half-hot pies also,
These ould deep-fryin' pans and fast food vans are the gourmet's overthrow.

This fast-food stuff is all the go as any schoolchild knows,
With stainless steel at every meal and tables in neat rows;
Kebabs and burgers thick with grease go sliding down young throats,
While Pizza Kings, and onion rings, the growing body bloats.

Now you will find, as I'll remind, at many of these stalls
The toxic smell of burning oil upon your senses palls,
While beneath your feet, upon the street, quite plainly to be seen
Are the remains of spuds and cardboard tubs and meat that's turning green.

Now it is a pleasant pastime if you have the time to spare,
To stand a while at such a place all for to gawk and stare,
Just to observe your neighbours with their bellies full of stout
Crying: "Two burgers there—th'oul' Miracle spare,
One with and one without!"

Like hurlers just outside the goal they jostle and they push,
They loudly cry and madly vie for all this instant mush;
And when in hand this drooling band discard without a care,
Those plastic forks and plastic box, the tools of this vile fare.

Oh Ireland, Mother Ireland, what has become of you?
Give us back our pots of coddle and our bowls of Irish stew.
You've replaced our rippling muscle with reams of rolling fat
By eating stuff that near enough you wouldn't feed your cat.

Oh, McDonald Mór, a curse on you, down in history you will go
For the increasity in obesity from eating your oul' dough.
Oh Pizza Hut and BurgerLand, you've rounded my slim waist,
On yous I blame this overhang composed from flour and paste.

So come all you healthy Irishmen, these mistakes do not be makin',
Short life preclude, fast food exclude, don't forsake your hairy bacon;
And you must chew raw turnips too, in your colon they won't lie,
For if you do not it'll be your lot to tumble down and die.

© Tim Lyons. This song can be heard on the album Big Guns and Hairy Drums.

Food songs seem rarely to have been written in praise of over-eating; rather they come from a period when hunger was common, and eating too much was a fantasy, a demonstration of wealth, and therefore, begrudgingly, something to be ridiculed. There are many variations on the theme of this one, a version of which I remember sung in Armagh by Johnny Murphy, a big man, as "The Big Feed". Expertise in construction and crafting have been surrendered in this case to the surreal—probably the product of the author's starvation hallucinations. In the quest to find something—anything—to rhyme, the bardic skills occupy only a mediocre plinth.

***

The Irish Jubilee

A short time ago, boys, an Irishman named Herrity
Was elected to the senate by a very large majority.
He felt so elated that he went to Denis Cassidy,
A man who owned a building of a very large capacity.
He says to Cassidy, "Go over to O'Leary
For a thousand pounds of chewing gum and give it to the poor,
Then go over to the butcher shop and order up a ton of meat;
Be sure the boys and girls have all they want to drink and eat.

Send out invitations in twenty different languages,
Don't forget to tell them to remember to bring sandwiches.
They made me their senator and so to show my gratitude
They'll have the finest supper ever given in this latitude.
Tell them the music will be furnished by O'Rafferty
Assisted on the uilleann pipes by Felix McCafferty.
Whatever the expenses are, remember I'll put up the tin,
And anyone who doesn't come be sure don't let them in."

Cassidy at once sent out the invitations
And everyone that turned out was a credit to their nations;
Some came on bicycles because they had no fare to pay,
And those who didn't come, made up their minds to stay away.

Two by three they marched into the dining hall,
Young men, old men, girls who were not men at all,
Single men, double men, men who had their teeth in pawn,
Blind men, deaf men and men who had their glasses on.

Before many minutes every chair was taken
Till the front rooms and mushrooms were packed to suffocation.
When everyone was seated they started to lay out the feast,
Cassidy says, "Rise up and give us each a cake of yeast."
He then said, "As manager he would try and fill the chair
And we all sat down and we looked at the bill of fare:
There was pigs' head, goldfish, mockingbirds and ostriches,
Ice cream, cold cream, Vaseline and prepostriches;

Bluefish, greenfish, fish hooks and partridges,
Fish balls, snow balls, cannonballs and cartridges;
We ate oatmeal till we could hardly stir about,
Catsup, hurry up, sweet kraut and sauerkraut,
Dressed beef, naked beef, beef with all its tresses on,
Sody crackers, firecrackers, Limberg cheese with dressing on,
Beef steak and mistakes were down the bill of fare,
Roast ribs, spareribs and ribs we couldn't spare;

Reindeer, snowdeer, deer meat and antelope,
The women ate mushmelon, the men ate cantaloupe,
Red herring, smoked herring, herring from old Erin's Isle,
Bologna, fruit cake, and sausages a half a mile;
There was hot corn, cold corn, corn salve and honeycomb,
Reed birds, read books, sea bass and sea foam,
Fried liver, baked liver, Carter's little liver pills—
Everyone was wondering who was going to pay the bill.

For dessert we had toothpicks, ice picks and skipping rope.
We washed them all down with a big piece of shaving soap.
We ate everything that was down on the bill of fare
And then looked on the back of it to see if any more was there.
The band played hornpipes, gas pipes and Irish reels.
We danced to the music of the wind that shakes the barley fields.
And the piper played old tunes and spittoons so very fine,
And when we paid the piper we handed him a glass of wine.

They welted the floor till they were heard for miles around.
When Ganniger was in the air, his feet were never on the ground.
A finer lot of dancers you never sat your eyes upon,
And those who couldn't dance at all were dancing with their slippers on:
Some danced jig steps, door steps and highland fling
Murphy took his knife out and tried to cut the pigeon wing.
And when the dance was over, Cassidy he told us
To join hands together and sing the good old chorus:

Should ould acquaintance be forgot
Wherever we may be,
Think of the good old times we had
At the Irish jubilee.

The wedding guest-list is second in importance only to the deceased's will in all human experience; those who are not included are presumed to have been deliberately excluded. But while with a will one must allow for a certain level of forgetfulness on the part of an aged elder, nevertheless there may well be a very good excuse for the paranoia of the victim of the wedding-list exclusion. Revenge would naturally be on the slighted one's mind and, if they were of lyrical bent, satire might set in. But "where could the song be sung?" is a reasonable question—unless the victim wished to bring on further exclusions. Of course if the lyrics were lacerating and mortifying enough then such feasts could become a guaranteed component of the scribe's future diet. This song was obviously written before the days of the motor car or bus, but not too early for the tune 'Moll Roe' (first noted in the mid nineteenth century) to be known. Baltray is a small village on the mouth of the river Boyne, east of Drogheda, Co. Louth, late 1800s. It was written by John Shiel, a local poet with an output of remarkable scope and quality, and was collected from Mary Ann Carolan (Usher) by Sean Corcoran, issued on the LP *Songs from the Irish Tradition*. Corcoran notes: "As well as their other shortcomings, the poet attributes to the guests socially inferior tastes in food—rayfish, hearts, goats' kidneys, lights and pigs' croobs. (It seems strange to the modern ear to hear veal included in this list!)".

***

Sweet Baltray

(Air: 'Moll Roe')

It was in the pleasant summer time
I roved along the river Boyne
To take the air I was inclined,
Oh nature seemed so gay;
And as I walked I chanced to meet
A friend sincere that did me greet
Who straightly asked me, most discreet,
To come to sweet Baltray.

I then complied with his demand,
He gave me sure to understand
His uncle's son would give his hand
Upon that very day;
And in wedlock bands he would be tied
Unto a brisk and virtuous bride,
And it's at the fun we would preside
That night in sweet Baltray.

But to pool force we did agree
And pace the road bein' full of glee
This pleasant pastime for to see
Without the least delay.
And at length we arrived at this swishful place
Where nuptial joys they filled each face,
We welcomed were to mirth and feast
That night in sweet Baltray.

Young Larkhill Dick with nosey Kate
Attended at the marriage treat
And mangy Ned with his bald pate
Came there with Nell McKay;
And Larkhill Dick and blind Moll Brown
And Peg McShane from Mornington,
They made the jovial toast go round
That night in sweet Baltray.

Now the groom was called ould Súgán Jack,
He had a horrid humpy back,
His teeth were rotten blue and black,
His eyes were shinin' grey;
And to crown the joke his nose was big
Likewise he wore a frizz of wig,
He snored and grunted like a pig
That night in Sweet Baltray.

The bride was aged about sixty-three,
She had one leg off above the knee,
Without a guide she couldn't see
To walk the King's highway;

And besides she had a monstrous scab
With a wild itch that's twice as bad,
Her equal sure could not be had
That night in Sweet Baltray.

To close the matrimonial knot
This charming pair it was up they got,
The words was said upon the spot,
At which all cried "Hooray!"
Then the people wished them all good joy
And every year a darlin' boy,
The bride she winked and did reply,
"Success to sweet Baltray!"

Good Irish whiskey was produced
At which MacShane he did play loose.
Says blear-eyed Bab: "By God I love the juice
Of barley every day!"
Says mangy Ned to Larkhill Dick
"I'm sure we both will love this trick:
We'll drink all night—suppose we're sick,
And ne'er can leave Baltray?"

The weddin' supper bein' served out,
Both right and left the play devoured,
You'd laugh to see their greasy snouts
Be smeared with big buck ray and trout,
And stay inclined to laugh and spake
The truth, with ling, cod, plaice and hake,
The roarin' doins they made them quake
That night in sweet Baltray.

There was assortments of fresh meat
For those who wished the same to eat,
Hearts, lights and skirts lay on each plate
Though no-one dare say "Nay!"
Pig's cheeks and croobs and fine fed veal
And nice goat's kidneys large and stale
And dumplins made of oaten meal
That night in sweet Baltray.

The bride and groom they did suggest
That they would really do their best,
They'd up and put them to the test
A few steps to display;
So mangy Ned tuned up his trump[38]
And Súgán Jack he shook his hump,
Lame Nan bate time with her horrid stump
That night in sweet Baltray.

'Moll Roe' was the only tune,
This couple jigged about the room,
Jack lorded like a bee in June
And Nan said, "Lave me way.
For when I get straight upon me prop
I'll hit the loft with every hop,
For, neighbours dear, I'm in me shop
This night in sweet Baltray!"

We all stood up unto give thanks
Oul Nan surprised and acted pranks,
Says Jack, "Me love, your nimble shanks
Would surely bear the sway
Of any thing I ever seen
Acted on stage or flowery green.
Oh was I king, you should be queen
This night in sweet Baltray."

The bridesmaid bein' a little tore
She gave a most tremendous roar
And said she'd sing a third encore
And drive all care away.
So when she coughed and cleared her throat
Her voice exceeded ass or goat;
She sang 'Moll D'alton' all by note.
We smiled in sweet Baltray.

Says mangy Ned to Blind Moll Brown,
"Tell Kate to put the kettle on."
Sweet nosey never seemed to frown
But straight away did obey.

Then a good strong tay each drank a quart,
The bride she swore it roused her heart,
Says "Jack, my love, I'll take your part
This night in Sweet Baltray."

I stood for ages for to view
This comic jovial hearty crew
For in all me life I never knew
A company so gay;
For some told stories, most sang songs,
And more of them danced and waltzed along;
The bagpipes sounded clear and strong
That night in sweet Baltray.

With tranquil pleasure and delight
And matchless fun we spent the night;
We clapped and cheered with all our might
Till near the break of day.
So Jack and Nan away were led
And instantly were put to bed;
We all shook hands and away we fled,
Away from sweet Baltray.

The Highlands and Islands Development Board in the 1990s was to the remote Scottish agricultural economy what the EC is to disadvantaged Ireland. Schemes to extract money are hatched by the hour, and people can spend their entire youth dreaming up ways to become rich. The most fertile soil for imaginative plantation is watered with whisky, and the best incubator for the tender seedlings is a bar. And none better than Andy Wilson's Fúarán Bar in the beauty spot Achiltiebuie (ach-ilty-boo-eee), north of Ullapool in the west north west of Scotland. Over a feast of the Fúarán's cucumber-sized prawns, transported on their final journey by a golden substance from an Old Inverness bottle no doubt, one dark winter's night Gairloch songwriter Andy Mitchell heard mumblings from a huddle of conspirators round the turf fire. They had just been watching a Russian-dubbed tape of Wild Bill Hickock that Andy had been given on a Soviet trawler as payment for fixing the radar. If the Wild West could have buffalo, then why not the West of Scotland? The best part of the scheme turned out to be the song, as is often the case with innovation, and it gave Andy a BBC prize and the opportunity to become famous and leave him giddy enough to have the confidence to go and turn around and give up his good job.

***

The Buffalo Farm in Achiltiebuie

(Air: 'Home on the Range')

OH!
The pies are fine and the meat's quite chewy
On the buffalo farm in Achiltiebuie
Run by Big Neil and wee S'Hughie,
Home on the range.

CHORUS:
Oh…Oh…Oh…Oh,
The pies are fine and the meat's quite chewy
On the buffalo farm in Achiltiebuie
Run by Big Neil and wee S'Hughie,
Home on the range.

In Achiltiebuie you won't get far
Without buffalo banging into your car
Especially if you've been to the Fúarán Bar,
Home on the range.
CHORUS

Now, the Chinese like their prawn chop suey,
The French they like their ratatouille,
But in Achiltiebuie that's far too gooey,
Home on the range.
CHORUS

At night the rustlers come in from the Glens,
A hairy band of Highland men
Led by a hombre called Iain MacBain,
Home on the range.
CHORUS

Now, the average weight of a buffalo
Is much the same as your Hielan' coo
So they've crossed them and called them *Beef-aloo,*
Home on the range.

Such a sight you'll never see
Wild buffalo all roamin' free,
And all on a grant from the HIDB, [39]
Home on the range.

© Andy Mitchell

There's plenty of talk about smoking and over-drinking in these islands. But over in the alleged 'land of the free' in the USA, in some places you could nearly get shot for such obscene activities in the 1980s. And if we are to read correctly the banning of smoking on long flights there, and the criminalization of smoking all over Europe we can expect to soon see smokers banned from entering the USA at all. But over there it's food a lot of unfortunate creatures seem to have a problem with. Probably they are of Famine-Irish extraction and are catching up. Crawford Howard observed the condition while on a mission there once and thought it would make a good recitation, but since he wanted to be able to come back to America he located it in Belfast.

***

The Foodaholic

There once was an ould alcoholic that lived up the Cliftonville Road
Whose behaviour was so diabolic—he never left till he was throwed
Out of every pub in the district. The doctor said, "If you don't stop
Inside six months at the latest, you'll definitely be for the chop."
Now this scared the oul eejit stupid, so he never went into a pub.
The funny thing was, like, whatever the cause, like—
He began to get drunk on his grub.

Now this was a strange situation: if he got a mouthful of tay,
Or a good bowl of soup, his head started to droop,
And the wife would say, "Gawd! He's a-way!"
Says the wife one night, "See thon oul geezer?
I'd like to get him by the hair,
For he stood my oul eegit an onion
And now he's away on the tare.
You know where I found the oul geezer? That full he couldn't half stand—
Lyin, across a deep freezer, with a fish finger stuck to his hand."

Then he fell into bad company, and he met an oul fool like his-self.
They got rotten on jelly and custard, and whatever he pinched off the shelf.
They'd get themselves bagfuls of toffee, sit gettin' plastered all day,
Standin' each other black coffees, fightin' about which one would pay.

They were soon known all round the district
And thought it was terrible hard
That if they went in to get a wee fish supper
They were always told, "Sorry, yis are barred."
The poor Chinese waiters were worried, they all knew what to expect—
If your boys'd had the chow mein and curry
They knew that the place would get wrecked.
One night your men overdone it—
They had two pasties over the eight
And they borrowed a car to get home like
For they knew it was terrible late.
Of course they were stopped by the Polis
And they started to shout and to barge.
"Youse have both overdone it this time
You're arrested for bein' drunk in charge."
The oul fella stood up in court like:
"We have this rap bate. Yis have made the charge sheet all wrong like—
We weren't drunk—we were ATE!

You'll still see them most Sunday mornin's
Bangin' the grocer's back door,
Standin' about, with their tongues hangin' out,
Just waitin' to get in for the cure.

© *Crawford Howard. This song can be heard on Crawford Howard's album* *The Diagonal Steam Trap.*

Part 10: Jesusry and Stuff

There is another side to hunger too, the political, and even religious.
Between 1847 and 1901, a result of famine and disease, eviction and
emigration, export of food and import of soldiers, the Irish
population decreased by as much as four million, leaving behind a deep
psychic scar with which our political process is still bound up. In the midst
of starvation in Somalia in the early 90s it seemed outrageous to see the
'warlords' roaming the streets in pickups mounted with cannon, well fed,
while thousands died each week for want of minimum calories. Josef Stalin
allegedly took all the food from the Ukraine in the 1920s to feed the
proletariat elsewhere (and to discourage secession by Ukraine) thus causing
the famine in which six million died. Famine Ireland also had such
incongruity, so it seems reasonable to conclude that famines are largely a
management issue, involved with degrees of loyalty to political hierarchies.
In famine Ireland, charities were at work dispensing soup to the starving.
Many of these were protestant religious foundations, Quaker etc. who
normally proselytised, and some increased their efforts during the famine.
In the winter of 1846-47 the first state 'soup kitchens' were opened for the
poor, as was, by a strange twist, the first Bewley's Cafe in Dublin for the rich.
In spring 1849 the Bible-thumping (and unfortunately-christened) RC.
Dallas opportunely set up the Society for Irish Church Missions to Roman

Catholics, and the story went round that the poor could get a meal or some clothes if they jumped the fence. The rumour, or fact, persists to this day. Protestant people, north and south, who have an obviously "Catholic", Irish, name are referred to as having "took the soup"[40]. The following song appeared in a collection of come-all-ye's in the USA in 1901, and is a cynical look at those who sampled the Campbell's to stay alive. For a change it is to the women that the responsibility for the upholding of faith and fatherland is being addressed…but then food and clothes are involved. Ted Hickey of Belfast used to sing this song to the air of The Ould Orange Flute. The chorus commemorates onetime US President Ronald Reagan's suspicious claim to be descended from famine Irish. This version is courtesy of Jane Flynn of Miltown Malbay.

***

Rigged Out

(Air: 'Mick Sullivan's Clock')

I'm a brand from the burnin'—a regular saint,
Newly purged and set free from Papistical taint;
Yes I'm one of that holy, that sanctified troop,
Whose souls have been chastened by flannel and soup—
Raddle Reagan-I, Reagan-I, Reagan-I, O.

I'll tell how so blessed a change came about,
For I always was lazy, a slouch and a lout;
I never was willin' to delve or to dig,
But I looked for support to me wife and the pig—
Raddle Reagan-I, Reagan-I, Reagan-I, O.

My spirit was never confused or perplexed
By the talk in this world about things in the next,
But I knew I'd be certain of one life of bliss
If someone would feed me for nothing in this—
Raddle Reagan-I, Reagan-I, Reagan-I, O.

And so by a ditch near my cabin I lay
With my front to the sun on a hot summer's day
When the Reverend Oliver Stiggins came by
And attracted my gaze by the whites of his eyes—
Raddle Reagan-I, Reagan-I, Reagan-I, O.

He addressed me and says, "I perceive by your face,
Wretched man, that you're much unacquainted with grace."
"Very true, sir," says I, "sure I scarce know the taste
Of the broth or the flesh of a four-footed baste"—
Raddle Reagan-I, Reagan-I, Reagan-I, O

Then he bade me arise and proceed with him home
Till he'd show me the proof of the errors of Rome.
I went, and the clincher that Oliver chose
Was a full and complete suit of second-hand clothes.
Raddle Reagan-I, Reagan-I, Reagan-I, O.

I felt at the moment the britches went on
That half of my ancient religion was gone.
Much was done by a vest buttoned up to the throat,
But the grand hit of all was a rusty black coat—
Raddle Reagan-I, Reagan-I, Reagan-I, O.

The hat was convincing—as one might expect—
And the necktie itself had a certain effect,
But to cut any error right out at the roots
He covered my croobs with a new pair of boots—
Raddle Reagan-I, Reagan-I, Reagan-I, O.

Then he raised up his eyes and his hands and began
To declare through his nose I'd put off the Old Man,
And he hoped to my newly-found faith I'd hold fast
Which I said that I would while his garments would last—
Raddle Reagan-I, Reagan-I, Reagan-I, O.

Then he bade me to speak unto Biddy my wife
About ribbons and cotton and Protestant life
And to ask her—with dear Mrs. Stiggins's regards—
What stuff would convert her, and how many yards—
Raddle Reagan-I, Reagan-I, Reagan-I, O.

I rushed home to Biddy, she shrieked with the fright;
She laughed till she wept at the comical sight.
She called me an *asal,* a rogue and a fool
And fell combing my head with a three-legged stool...
Raddle Reagan-I, Reagan-I, Reagan-I, O.

She threw me right out and she bolted the door.
I kicked and I shouted, I cursed and I swore.
Ah, but soon I grew weak when it came to my mind—
I could fare very well, leavin' Biddy behind...
Raddle Reagan-I, Reagan-I, Reagan-I, O.

From town until town I have travelled since then
Givin' good British scripture to women and men,
And if at times I indulge in a sexual freak—
Sure doesn't Stiggins himself know—the flesh is but weak...
Raddle Reagan-I, Reagan-I, Reagan-I, O.

The 1980s were full of debates on women in (or rather not in) the Churches. But in '86 the Vatican got around to talking about it and the lads there decided among themselves that the idea of women priests was really quite preposterous—if Jesus had wanted women priests he would have been a woman, wouldn't he? (Lawyers for the clerical defence might say that though he had the power to make a Toyota, yet he rode a donkeY, so the club remains men only among the Catholic, while other denominations have got women bishops and priests). The incident that provoked this song was the Catholic bishops' seminar in September '86 where one of the topics for tortured discussion was "Does the TV viewer of the Pope's blessing get the same indulgence[41] as the person on the ground who witnesses it live in St. Peter's Square?" And further—the discussion developed—"Does a person who watches a video recording of the Pope's blessing get the same indulgence?" It took a clever man to find that loophole. Churches are like Political systems—you can never win: even when you spend all your money on video machines to avoid 'doing your time', they go and slap you in the face by making a new rule. In the end they decided on a compromise—you get the indulgence the first time you see the blessing on the box, and not again. (But what if you watched him give it in all sorts of different places, say on a world multi- stop tour? And what if you're not a Catholic—does it work anyway?) And these were grown men. No wonder we have to write songs.

***

The Genesis Song

(Air: 'Dan O'Hara')

Well, good evenin' ladies—won't yis to my pulpit draw up near
And stay awhile to hear me ex-pla-na-a-tion
As to how, why, when and where all religions have such fear
Of the women bein' let into ordination.

You see it all goes back to space, to long before the human race,
When God was the star of genetic engin-e-eer-in'.
On one unproductive day, he made a man from bits of clay
And popped him into his safari ga-ar-den.

This was fine for many years—there were no arguments or tears,
Or any big emotional com-pli-ca-a-tions,
Till one day while father played with young Adam's bones he made,
By accident, the female of the spe-e-cies.

For a whole day all went grand, but when night fell Eve could not stand,
This thing that we call sex-u-al frus-tra-a-tion,
Caused by yelps and squeaks and sighs, grunts and gasps and happy cries
Of the birds and beasts in joyous proc-re-a-a-tion.

So when she got up Eve said, "Fuck this, for a lark—look what we miss,
By not givin' into our temp-ta-a-tion."
She took a wise ould snake's advice, a-and after several tries
She invented heterosexual re-la-a-tions.

When he heard this, father blew his top and says, "You two,
Have made me the laughin' stock of animation.
If we had neighbours what would they say? If youse had mothers
     they'd be disgra-ced,
So I'm barrin' youse for breach of regulations."

We've all been cursed since then by women's seduction worked on men;
You can see the stories daily in the papers:
Saucy bishops, vicars and priests, on the go like heinous beasts,
We have to disenchant them from this caper.

So today we keep alive our resistance as we strive
To make amends for Adam's in-dis-crè-è-tion.
So we're celibate and live in a secret society run by men
To control the consequences of the wee-e-min.

In our synods and seminars and our councils we have barred
Participation by you gentle cray-ay-tures.
You're not endowed by God to make proclamations o-on sex,
On contraception, marriage, land or nature.

So only men still can debate if indulgence is a state
That can be transferred or not by tele-vi-i-sion,
Or if angels still have wings, are boys, or girls—or things—
And the size we should be makin' eyes in nee-ee-dles.

Don't be such begrudgers, trust us trained the-ologians, we'll explain
How faith in us insures re-in-car-na-a-tion.
You, just give up your name and praise Allah, Buddha, Lord, or Jaze-
Us Christ and we'll save you from your dam-na-a-tion.

© *Fintan Vallely*

Living so far from the 'Holy Land' as we do here in Ireland, we tend to make a national compensation for that fact by being extremely dedicated to the active pursuit of Christianity. This is done often in a manner which suggests that either it is the only religion in the world, or it is the best religion in the world. Television refutes any questions about the first possibility; crusades and war-mongering illustrate that there is at least a major flaw in the second. In any case, even the otherwise foolish, ignorant, anti-intellectual and travel-phobic in our most backward urban and rural midst can work up a lump in the throat over events which began in Palestine a couple of thousand years ago. One of the stories from those momentous biblical times which is particularly delighted in in Ireland—being paid tribute to indeed by the exercise of forty days and nights of going off sweets by children (and cigarettes and drink when you're big)—is how Jesus predicted his own death, how he was betrayed, was given a hard time, rejected by Myles na Gopaleen's 'plain people', hung on a cross beside the General Lennie Murphy and Gerry Adams, and let die.

The death bit was public, but the resurrection was behind closed doors, so to speak, and consequently we are all expected to take his word for it and believe in it even though we never met him (this is 'the faith'). There is a certain scope for doubt; for instance Thomas questioned it all—and he KNEW Jesus. The truth of the matter is that it was a publicity stunt that went wrong—like having a Falklands, 'Gulf' or Iraq war without CNN. Jesus did want coverage; Peter mucked it up, and his boss was so pissed off that he only made a couple of token appearances to the Lads afterwards and eventually went back to heaven.

The apostles, as everybody knows, were heavily into Irish music and they liked a couple of drinks of a weekend—especially with a Bank Holiday coming up. Christy Moore told this story in joke form one Good Friday while locked in in Friel's of Miltown Malbay. When eventually the call came from RTÉ to do a song for *The Sunday Show* on Easter Sunday morning of 1990 I knew this was my moment—I converted the joke into a song. Producer Noel Coughlan wasn't pleased, nor was presenter Andy O'Mahoney: they decided that their show was a "family" one, and the Irish public weren't ready for this kind of thing yet, in spite of the success of *Jesus Christ Superstar* (the things 'the family' is accused of these days). *The Missing Missus* song was the second runner, but at the last minute it was given the thumbs down too. Easter is Easter. Christianity is Christianity. Ireland was born of an Easter Sunday and we appear to be mostly Christians. (Salman Rushdie wasn't mentioned but I'd read the papers). This is the true story in song. The air is *The Granemore Hare,* a song set around Keady in Co. Armagh.

125

The Resurrection Romp

(Air: 'The Granemore Hare')

One eve-nin' in April Christ called in the lads
To take urgent note of a new scheme he had:
"Th'oul fella tould me when I phoned home
That from Good Friday on youse are out on your OWN,
COCKA DOODLE I DOODLE I DOODLE I DAY."

"Now, Peter my dear fri-e-nd, please pay close heed,
For what's goin' down's a bit hard to believe.
In a nutshell, quite shortly, I won't be with ye—
For the da has decided to sacrifice ME,
COCKA DOODLE I DOODLE I DOODLE I DAY."

"Ah, Jasis, come off it, you're soft in the head,
Sure a grand healthy young lad like you won't be dead
For at least forty years, you've a fine life ahead—
Cheer up, and we'll go for a drink in Mc—DAID'S
COCK A DOODLE I DOODLE I DOODLE I DAY."

"Look, Pete, settle down, this is what it entails—
And if it doesn't happen my mission will fail:
On Friday at three I die aft'r a par-ade—But
On Sunday, the deal is, I rise from the—DEAD,
COCKA DOODLE I DOODLE I DOODLE I DAY."

"Ah, Jay, you're the divil! But you know I care,
And you know that I'd follow you anywhere.
But 'RESS'RECTION', y'ould cod—now you're pushin' me there!
Oh, the THINGS you come out with, by Christ you're a—RARE—ONE,
COCK DOODLE I DOODLE I DOODLE I DAY."

"PETER!—Quit messin! All this is true,
A-a-nd for the P-R, I'm depending on you
Come Sunday at dawn, I'll emerge from the to—oomb
I want to see CNN, Charlie Bird and Sky NEWS—
COCKA DOODLE I DOODLE I DAY."

Well, next thing he was lifted, and couldn't get bail,
And under the PTA locked up in jail
On the word of some Phar'see' in *The Times* or *The Mai-l,*
Was sentenced to hang from a cross by three—NAILS—
COCKA DOODLE I DOODLE I DOODLE I DAY."

Du—uly two mornin's later before the sun rose
He was up and about practis'n media pose-
Ing and drafting press statements in BBC prose,
To explain why an East-er uprising was chose -EN,
COCK DOODLE I DOODLE I DOODLE I DAY.

A—at six on the button, he rolled back the stone,
But to his dismay not a sinner had shown;
Not a soul was in sight, no witness was there—
But by sounds from the town they were out on the—TEAR—
COCKA DOODLE I DOODLE I DOODLE I DAY.

In the BÉAL BOCHT he tripped over Simon and Bat,
Who said: "Try the FOUR SEASONS for Taddeus and Matt."
John, Andy and Phil raved in MOTHER RED CAP—'s
In the BRAZEN-HEAD Judas was knockin' back— SCHNAPPS—
COCKA DOODLE I DOODLE I DOODLE I DAY.

A supergrass at the 'MEETING PLACE' led him to HUGH's-IS
Where Thomas was doubting the wisdom of booze-
Ing, the James' mauled Guinness in O'DONOG-HUE'S
While the Góilín had Peter up singing,
"COCK DOO- COCK A DOODLE I DOODLE I DOODLE I DAY."

"Ah, Jasus!" says Peter, "Well, you know what it is!"
"You'll be ragin' you died when you hear what you missed:
Judas came home on Wed-ens-day night with a fist-
Full of silver and since then we've been on the—PISS—
COCKA DOODLE I DOODLE I DAY."

*'The Granemore Hare', which provides the air for this song, can be heard
on Kevin Mitchell's Greentrax album I Sang The Sweet Refrain.*

There have been two hundred and fifty reported Christian apparitions in the last fifty years world wide. But since most of them have not been sanctioned by the Catholic Church authorities, so therefore they didn't happen. In March 1985 two schoolchildren in Asdee, Co. Kerry saw a Virgin and (her) child (statue) move in their local chapel. As a result Ireland bate England at rugby, and, so encouraged, by the year's end in twenty-six places with all sorts of unsavoury names like 'Ball in spittle' previously content and immobile (females all) statues of stone, plaster and reinforced concrete began to move—wink, weep, bleed, sigh, talk and even light up. The thing caught on like good scandal and became Ireland's only growth industry of the 80s. Pilgrims mobbed the shrines to stand for hours in the incessant rain. Tour buses, Telecom workers, and car-park tarmacadamers made a bomb. Burger, chip and ice-cream vans and Portaloo suppliers flocked to service the hungry hordes while the relic, statuette, plastic Jesus, snowstorm St. Bernadette, rosary bead, holy picture and prayerbook floggers got a share of the action too, giving the grottos the air of the marketplace in *Jesus Christ Superstar*. Colm Tóibín somehow got a book out of it and Nell McCafferty pondered the curious fact that the statues had only moved in the 26 Counties.[42] (Perhaps the ones in the North were afraid to move?). But the supernatural was indeed at work quietly up there—for at around the same time someone in West Belfast saw the face of Jesus in a Grecian tile fireplace one night after confusing that device with a mirror. Thousands queued up, causing consternation among soldiers who raided the house thinking it might be giving out guns; the Provos too investigated, thinking that it might be dealing in drugs.

In civilised America in 1993, I was assured by a woman driving a $30,000 car that a friend of a friend of a friend of her friend's friend had had her Connamara marble rosary beads turned to solid gold by a statue in Maryland (typical of greedy America—when it's Connamara itself that needs those sort of skills badly all they got was a blubberer, and they lost the gold contract too). Headlines in *America Today* magazine showed that a priest in new Jersey had not just one weeping Madonna on his hands, but every time he entered a room with a statue or a holy picture the whole lot would go off like the photo-electric gushers in a men's urinal. And somewhere in the former Yugoslavia hordes flock to look at the vision of Christ in a wonky glass pane. Religious authorities sensibly hold that this is all rubbish, and that if people want to have faith they should have it in their bricks and mortar religion (because that's the only thing that is of any economic value to their clergy in this world). Co-incidentally, 1985 saw the last car assembled in Ireland, was the occasion of a dreadful wet summer, the year of the first mention of a referendum on Divorce, and the moment of change in contraception laws. The statues were jumping for joy and weeping with relief that at long last things were different. In the end they opted to play with the audiences just like politicians—keep them waiting and keep them guessing. So frustrating was that experience for some grottophiles that they attacked the more cynical statues with hatchets and lump hammers. But if that all appears a bit absurd, just think of those milk-supping statues all over the Hindu world and in India: would it be possible that people could start feeding water to crucified Jesuses, or stout to the Father Matthew statue in Cork?

A few songs emerged out of the hoo-hah, but the apparition at Knock, the grandmammy of them all, in July 1879 had already laid the foundation. This too occurred after a summer of solid rain[43] in the year of the worst harvest since the big famine years of the 1840s, in the midst of evictions, in the teeth of rows over protestant soul-saving in neighbouring Galway, and four days after the founding of The Land League in Mayo. It created the Irish statue industry as we know it today, and without it the relapse of 1985 and the songs which follow would have been impossible. The Pope visited the site a hundred years later but he saw nothing.

∗∗∗

The Moving Statues Movement
(Air: 'We Shall Not Be Moved')

We're on our way to freedom, we've nothin' left to lose,
Fed up with adoration, to move is what we choose;
It's like a Friday night in Glenamaddy[44] when the statues move,
For we are the statues, statues on the move.
We're the movin' statues movement and to move is what we choose;
It's like a Friday night in Glenamaddy when the statues move.

From outside every chapel, perched on altars and on walls,
From roadside, school and mantelpiece, we've answered all your calls;
We're sick of unpaid workin' at idolatry, we want to be free,
We all want, we want to be free.
We're the movin' statues movement and we move that we be free,
We're sick of unpaid workin' at idolatry, we want to be free.

For years youse foolish people have flocked in hordes to Rome
To gawp at shameless lazy lumps of marble, brass and stone.
Come to us!—Just paint and plaster, but we bleed, convulse and glow—
We're Ireland's holy show.
We are the Irish, the Irish holy show,
Just one mention of divorce, our tears begin to flow;
Come to us, just paint and plaster, but we bleed, convulse and glow,
We're Ireland's holy show.

With some co-operation we'll contort to your commands,
But we want European clothes and mittens for our hands,
Index-linked donations, central heatin' for our stands,
Those are our demands.
There yis have them, those are our demands,
Grant them, and the movin' statues move to your commands;
Index-linked donations, central heatin' for our stands,
Those are our demands.

For we are the statues, statues on the move,
We're the movin' statues movement and to move is what we choose;
It's like a Friday night in Glenamaddy when the statues move.

© *Fintan Vallely. This song can be heard on the album* Big Guns and Hairy Drums. *The song is a parody of a Gospel hymn which has been used by almost every liberal and left political campaign and trade union since the 1940s.*

Continuing the saga of women in the Christian churches, in October 1989 the Church of England Primate Dr. Robert Runcie visited the Pope in Rome to sign some sort of cease-fire agreement. Irish interest in the affair concerns the fact that Ian Paisley was roaring outside the meeting about Runcie being an 'ecclesiastical Judas' and a 'crypto papist'. Sex came into it too, with journalist Nell McCafferty remarking that it was curious that Mrs. Runcie was nowhere to be seen in the proceedings which were heavily covered by television. It was concluded that the explanation for her absence must lie in the area of sex, because everything else about the two men was the same— manner of dress, hobbies, belief in the one God, etc.—and it could hardly have been because she was a Protestant. No, obviously Pope Paul had had a hard enough time living down the public image of some of his more illustrious predecessors, if not some of his subordinates, without being witnessed by the world's eye in the company of a woman who, by her title, brazenly professed her sexual relations with a bishop. While she was not in the habit of being out on safari with him ever—herself being a concert pianist—for the sake of this song it is presumed that Mrs. R. wasn't invited. Mind you there were so many gorgeous, embroidered garments being proudly sported by the ageing glitterati of Patriarchy that the press could be forgiven for missing a woman's presence. This song is about what really happened when the Pope found out that Mr and Mrs R. intended coming together.

***

The Missing Missus Mystery

(Air: 'Football Crazy' [45] *)*

We'll live in troubled times always, no matter what they say,
Of desire for 'normality' and Shangri-La some day,
But drugs and murder aren't my plot, right here I'll deal with sex
And how its absence in Church scenes has drastic side effects.

CHORUS:
For he's TV crazy, he's jet plane mad,
He's Perestroika-stricken, on a Lech Walesa fad.

Some choose to simply live alone and hold up heads in spite
Of pressure to have children who'd control their lives outright;
Some've one-night stands or live in sin but get on no-one's goat,
For they don't make religious rules and shove it down our throats.[46]
Oh he's CHORUS

There's others in our midst though whose right to work's from God,
Under fifty-seven labels that condense to Taig and Prod;
The Papish padrés can't have sex but the vicars can enjoy
Their faithful's favourite evening sport and still remain employed.

For He's...CHORUS

Now protestants are sensible, they know that legislate-ing
On fleshy things demands that you've no jealousy or hatred;
They let their clergy marry so that they can regulate
With intelligent experience their subject's loves and fates.

Still he's...CHORUS

And there's much afoot this weather in them Reformation churches.
Their inaugruatin' women priests leaves Catholics in the lurch.
They'd like to get together, agin' all non-Jesus hordes,
But there's women in their woodpile who aren't like 'yer wan' at Lourdes.

He's...CHORUS

So then on the big day that agreements were bein' signed
J.P. called his go-for in and says, "Zee bawtuhm lion
Ees trawkhingk veeth a Prawteshtant een frohnt off zeh tee fee,
Not haffingk meesus beeshop making meeky owt off mee."

For He's CHORUS

He bate the bed and threw the head round like a World Cup ball.
His hermit's mind was tortured by lewd thoughts of Adam's 'fall'.
"How vould vee noh eeef Rawhnsees hat eet ohff befohr zey callt—
Or maypee she'd vear troushers and maake eediotz off us ahl."

For He's...CHORUS

He's hugged Communist and heathen, Muslim, Hindu, Jew,
Even with his hit-man[47] he has had a rendezvous;
Indiscriminately round the world says, "Peep-hole aye laff hoo,"
But Missus Bishop Runcie dear, he drew the line at you.

For he's TV crazy, he's jet plane mad,
He's Perestroika stricken on a Lech Walesa fad;
Indiscriminately round the world says, "Peep-hole aye laff hoo."
But Missus Bishop Runcie dear, he drew the line at you.

© *Fintan Vallely. This song can be heard on archive tape
at the Irish Traditional Music Archive.*

Part 11: Lovers' Frolics

THE GLASGOW COURTSHIP

Aisling poetry from the end of 18th century was in common usage as songs moulded to suit the day and age. Some of these, aimed at the Munster masses, appeared in English on broadsides printed in Cork and Limerick. In them Ireland is supposed to have been portrayed as a *spéirbhean* (heavenly woman). But maybe they just wanted to write erotically and be safe from criticism by the clergy? Anyway, the thing was for the poet to show off skill and knowledge of the classics in the choosing of lyric questions designed to establish Her identity. The results could be quite amazing. Adam McNaughton, worn out by having to respond to requests for 'Carrickfergus', decided to create an opportunity to show off his own knowledge of the *aislingí*, the craft of the schoolmaster poet, the classics and certain realities about sensible women. An ideal song for anti-pretentious, parlour-party singers.

*** *

The Glasgow Courtship

(Air: 'Carrickfergus')

To Glasgow city when I first came o-o-ver
I took a walk in the pleasant south;
'Twas there I met a most beauteous cree-ee-ture,
A goddess fai-air in the bloom of youth;

134

I nothing po-on-dered, but to her wa-an-dered,
And thus addressed her: "Where do you dwell?
Is it Par-na-ssus or Halikarna-as-sus?"
Her modest answer was, "Away tae hell!"

Though something daunted, I remained encha-an-ted,
She was the fairest my eyes had seen.
"Are you Aurora or the goddess Flo-o-ra
Or of Caledonia its gracious queen?"
"It's a gude job for you that ah'm no Aur-o-or-a,
As you can tell by the way ah speak,
'Cos all them lassies from Halikarna-ass-us
They talk in Latin or in bloody Greek."

Then my third address it was the be-e-est:
"Of Scotia's beauties you are the queen."
"Ah, yer patter's muck—go gi'e it a chuck—
And try tae talk like a human bee-n.
Ma name is Sadie an' ah come frae Tradeston,
Yer very welcome tae come back to mine;
If you cut the blether we can get together
Over a Chinese carry-oot and a bottle a wine."

So come all ye bards of a high re-ga-a-ard
Who dip your pens in sweet Helicon's springs;
To Scotia's shore if you ramble o-o-wer
A different strai-ain I would have you sing.
For maids residing by the shores of Cly-y-yde
Will not be won by a honeyed line;
The only art to-o win their hea-a-arts
Is a bottle a' wannie[48] and chicken chow mein.

This can be heard on Adam McNaughton's Greentrax album Words I Used To Know. *The air of 'Carrickfergus' is on albums by many, including De Dannan, Brian Kennedy, Van Morrison and Dominic Behan.*

The town of Crossmaglen in south County Armagh is famous for the song *The Dalin*[49] *Men of Crossmaglen,* popularised by Tommy Makem in the 60s. It's also famous for the harbouring of a resentment over the way things turned out in 1921, and for the way the natives were perpetually microwaved by British Army radio monitors, infra-red scanning and electronic scouring of the airwaves. There, too, just as the 1994 cease-fires were announced, the BA went mad with security and refused to get off the football pitch that they'd occupied for years out of spite at not being able to win. In the middle of all this, John Garvey from Kiltibane used drop in to the Keenan sisters' pub in The Square where the great order kept was demonstrated by the presence of flowers. Observing the absence of these one day, he offered to rectify the deficit with some wild daffodils, but was unfortunately observed by the scribe Jim McAllister who turned around and wrote up the incident for the annals of history with a satirical nib.

***

The Daffodil Man From Kiltybane

(Air: 'Trippin' Up to Claudy', 'Banks of the Roses', etc.)

Armagh's the 'Orchard County', the home of honest men,
It runs from north of Lurgan town down south to Crossmaglen;
From County Down to the Monaghan hills, it stretches east to west,
With County Louth as it's southern friend and its north by Lough
    Neagh caressed.
Rally fol le deedle die doh, right fal the dee

Its name is steeped in history, St Patrick loved its soil.
It gave succour to the hunted, and the hunter its mountains foiled.
But it isn't my intention to sing all its praise in rhyme—
I'm telling a different story at this present point in time.
Rally fol le deedle die doh, right fal the dee.

I'm bringing to your notice a story of renown,
How a bunch of golden Daffodils arrived in our fair town.
On the square of Cross there stands a pub run by three lassies rare
And all the local bachelors by right assemble there.
Rally fol le deedle die doh, right fal the dee.

But alas, for all us single men, it's sad news that I tell,
For two of the women are married, and the other's promised as well.
We all had our chances of Bernadette's fair hand
Until we were outwitted by a ramblin' Daffodil man.
Rally fol le deedle die doh, right fal the dee.

Yes, the Daffodil man from Kiltybane, John Garvey is his name,
Got fed up with bein' single and planned to stake his claim;
He wooed the charming Bernadette with nods and winks and glances
And sometimes plucked up courage and met her at 'Blayney dances.
Rally fol le deedle die doh, right fal the dee.

But something still was lacking and yet she wouldn't say,
Then Garvey saw a notice about *The Interflora Way:*
"Say it with flowers!" the paper said, "That's the way to tell your love!"
"Be God," says John, "That's what I'll do for my wee turtle dove."
Rally fol le deedle die doh, right fal the dee.

But Kiltybane is a barren land that's full of bogs and rushes
Where the ragweed and the thistle grow among the blackthorn bushes,
Where the goats do search for a bite to eat upon it's miserable clay,
And snow can fall quite heavily—upon a Summer's day.
Rally fol le deedle die doh, right fal the dee.

The weeds grow in profusion and scutch grass is its sweetest flower,
And Garvey searched for blossoms there in vain for many hours;
At last the truth began to dawn and he gave up the search
And morbidly depressed went down to the lake to fish for perch.
Rally fol le deedle die doh, right fal the dee.

But as he sat there fishing a thought came to his mind
That daffodils in Sheetrim's hills he could surely find,
So he ran like hell from Kiltybane till Sheetrim he did spy,
And there miles and miles of golden daffodils did fill his loving eye.
Rally fol le deedle die doh, right fal the dee.

He plucked them with his toil-worn hands till he had a mighty bunch,
And going home contented he ate a hearty lunch.
That evening he came into the town his heart with love did beat
As he tried to hide the daffodils from people on the street.
Rally fol le deedle die doh, right fal the dee.

At last he came to Keenan's and Bernadette he saw,
And handed her his blossoms with a blush on his manly jaw.
The rest of us poor bachelors with envy just looked on
And Tom Lambe was swearing silently as he gazed with awe on John.
Rally fol le deedle die doh, right fal the dee.

The Duncans both were raging and McAllister had a fit
As he ordered up another Bush and on his tongue he bit;
Mulligan wouldn't speak at all and Casey downed his drink,
And poor heart-broken Anthony Shields couldn't even think.
Rally fol le deedle die doh, right fal the dee.

Rooney pondered on the case and said quite sorrowfully,
"There goes my dream of a pub in Cross, still single I must be."
The moral of this story, lads, would seem to go like this—
If you would go a courting, pluck flowers for your lass.
Rally fol le deedle die doh, right fal the dee.

And now this tale is over, but one thing's left unclear:
What will Thomas Henry do when the sad news he does hear?
That the Daffodil man from Kiltybane has won sweet Bernie's hand
And Garvey is the chosen one of Keenan's bachelor band.
Rally fol le deedle die doh, right fal the dee.

© Jim McAllister

In days before television, roads, records, transport, telephones, movies and money-to-spare, people stuck to their home patch. A visiting stranger might cause great excitement, the very idea of working for an industrial wage was captivating, the possibility of getting paid to join an army (depending on your political beliefs) fitted—or was moulded around—important notions of male valour. The visit of a regiment in glowing regalia, announced by the awesome flutes or brass of an ordered military band, must have been hugely alluring to the innocent among the drabness and hand-to-mouth subsistence of a rural life. Many lads joined up, many never returned, but going by ballad lyrics a promise was good enough to 'hold' a female partner on the home patch until 'Johnny's return in seven years or whatever. Sometimes of course the lovers might get married prior to his departure, but loneliness might get the better of the woman, she might get sick of the waiting and take up or off with another, wiser, local glamour boy.

And so the tale of the cuckolded soldier: himself joins up, cuts a fine dash in a bright uniform in order to impress his love, goes off to the wars, discovers why red was a good colour for the jackets, loneliness gets the better of the spouse. While some of the stories conclude on happiness—broken rings and beer mats matched up and reunited—others, like 'John Reilly' and 'Young Edmund', wind up in disaster. Bill Watkins, an eccentric wandering Scotsman, constructed this one out of old bits of internal rhyming after having being seduced, deuced and dumped by a publican's daughter. He now runs Merlin's Rest, a licensed premises in Minneapolis where he plays bagpipes and hosts Traditional music sessions.

***

The Errant Apprentice

When I was a young apprentice and less than *compos mentis*
I took leave of all my senses with a maid I fell in love;
Her ringlets so entwined me, Aphrodite's smile did blind me,
Cupid's arrow struck behind me, and her father owned a pub.
It was there I met my nemesis in her father's licensed premises,
Like the Seraphim of Genesis sat Mary Anne Maguire;
Arrayed in fine apparel, astride a porter barrel,
She looked the kind of girl that would fill you with desire.

All the turtle doves were cooing as I took to my wooing,
Her loveliness pursuing in the springtime that year,
But she thought I should be older and more gallant and much bolder,
In the uniform of a soldier 'tis then she'd hold me dear.
In extremis and euphoria I joined with Queen Victoria
For a spell of death or glory—ah, ah fighting with the Boers.
To the wind I threw all caution, I'll return with fame and fortune
And together make a portion of matrimony's chores.

On the gravestone of her mother she swore she loved no other,
But I was soon to discover that she played me for a jerk;
For lady luck had beached me and intelligence had reached me,
Whilst I'd been overseas she had got married to a Turk.
Well me, I then deserted for to find the girl who flirted,
Back to Ireland I reverted for my jealousy was roused;
In Maguire's pub in Derry, I found him making merry
With his arms around my Mary as together they caroused.

So I took my time and waited until his thirst was sated
And home he navigated through the streets of that walled town;
And at his lodgings he stood knocking and whilst they were unlocking,
I put a stone into a stocking, on his head I brought it down.
'Twas then the night's serenity was rent with loud obscenity
And Ottoman profanity that I couldn't understand;
With an oath he made to grab me, with full intent to stab me,
But as he tried to kebab me I was screaming up the strand.

All round the town's perimeter he chased me with his scimitar,
A powerful passion limiter to an errant in his pride;
Through the Waterside he chased me, to the bridge of Foyle he raced me,
And at Derry Quay he faced me so I jumped into the tide.
Sure bravery's no virtue when some ballox's tryin' to hurt you,
And all noble thoughts desert you when you see his curly knife;
For there's many things worth tryin' for, and occasionally worth lyin' for,
But there's bugger-all worth dyin' for, so I'll stick to the soldier's life.

© *Bill Watkins. This song can be heard on Andy M. Stewart's album,*
Man in the Moon.

Part 12: Matters Mundane

The Dentist from Fivemiletown

The barber in Afghanistan is considered to be the person woth the skills appropriate to dealing with all things to do with fighting such as hair, nails and teeth. Music was also considered to be one one his things, making his business a significant institution in any locality. Somewhere in the not-too-distant past, things weren't very different in the western world either, and barbers in the European wild west of the USA pulled teeth, making their institution a totally terrifying place. Prior to its demise after the invention of male vanity, the barber shop was the most rugged outcrop of maleness—a *temple* of maleness—for unlike the pub you absolutely had to go in at least once a month. Only males went in there, and they went in to have violence done to themselves in the approving environment of other males. It was an act of faith in consensus, for if the barber didn't like you or your family, all individuality and personality could be left behind on the floor and you could be humiliated for life: he had both the power to ruin or boost an individual's self-esteem, and the total control over how every male in the locality was going to be presented to the outside world.

The clientele too were a source of terror, whether you were just waiting, or trapped in the throne being studied and evaluated from all angles. You never knew who was going to be there, for there were always people in the queue. Nor did you know what the topic of conversation was going to be— cattle, horse-racing, cars, but maybe politics, drink, sex—or even you. The barber controlled this—but it was a battle of wits between his strength of personality and the sum total of that of the particular collection of customers at any moment. A man of power everyone feared slightly, and to whose weapon-wielding hands you entrusted your very life, he could fall in, initiate, reflect, discourage, derail, redirect or manipulate the mood just like a music hall master of ceremonies. Like the pubs too, each shop had its specific type of clientele, diluted by the odd 'outsider' or country child. As you entered this theatre you trembled, because depending on the composition of the assembled, your haircut experience could truly be a nightmare. And if it wasn't, you would be terrified that it might be. As a child though you were probably luckier than those getting a razor-shave—that was for the brave. For them a shave was dicing with death as the maestro swathed his way blind through the foam like a car at night plunging in an act of faith into the black hole to the left of a set of oncoming headlights, every accent and incident expanded and inscribed on the air by the cut-throat razor brandished in demonstrative or aggravated gesticulation around a stretched throat. Hugh Collins of Lisnaskea, who wrote up until his death in 1985 at age 92, put together the following account of dental expertise in a barber's shop in the early part of the century. Luckily for him the dentist's drill hadn't yet arrived.

***

The Dentist from Fivemiletown

(Air: 'The Garden Where the Praties Grow')

You meet with jolly fellows when abroad you chance to roam,
I suppose that is the reason why I seldom stay at home;
In our town, some time ago another friend I found,
The rarest gem I met for years who comes from Fivemiletown.

I was speaking to the barber and complaining of my jaws.
Says he, "Tis not the whiskers, but the teeth that are the cause.
If you call in on Tuesday night I've hit upon a plan,
For trouble of that nature mister Stansfield is your man."

When I called with the barber and the dentist was not in
I began to lose my patience and to curse I did begin.
When he arrived, I said, "Old man, what have you been about?
I've got some nasty molars that require hauling out."

142

He says, "What is the matter?" "To be candid I don't know,
But I fear I have some quare'ns that from the gums will have to go."
"Just wait a moment, sonny, and when I get looking through,
Depend on me, I'll quickly see what I can do for you."

"You have some teeth as black as coal and some are worn down,
Some like the leaves in Autumn they are turned a golden brown;
I've come to the conclusion there is not a shade of doubt,
The only patent for you is to have the beggars out."

It was then I prayed for Heaven where hard working fellas go,
I always dread the company and the climate down below.
In grief I thought of all my friends so jovial and so kind,
And I prayed for all the lady friends that I might leave behind.

He widened my receiver with his fingers and his thumbs,
Then he got his little oiler and began to oil my gums;
It was sharper than a British sword was made the Turks to kill,
And he used it like a peeler who was hunting for a still.

The little weary travellers that were resting in my hair
Got a snuff of Stansfield's stuff and were driven off their lair;
They were shocked beyond endurance and transported from their home,
And half a dozen passed away beneath my collar bone.

I had a curious feeling that I could not understand,
While my gums were fairly fizzing like a sausage in a pan.
You know this Clabby relish that I won't complain about
Has surely got a flavour I would rather do without.

The order then was "left", "incline", "keep steady in the chair!
"I cannot work the lever till your jaws are on the square."
He then produced as many tools and placed them in a row
As would pull a man asunder from the muzzle to the toe.

He got the tools in motion and evicted the amount—
The teeth fell out like paving stones until I lost the count—
Then asked me "Was it painful?" in a voice both low and kind.
I said, "I'll never grumble if you leave the jaws behind."

"Just take a little relish, son, you'll never feel the pain,
And when your gums are hardened up just toddle in again,
And I'll supply you with a set will last you all your life;
If she isn't gone before you, you can will them to your wife."

Success to Mister Stansfield that hero of renown,
A credit to the country and the pride of Fivemiletown;
This enemy of toothache to you all I recommend,
For after all is said and done he is the poor man's friend.

© *Hugh (the poet) Collins. Published in The Songs of Hugh the Poet by Patrick Collins*

Since there are songs about all other aspects of the human condition, why not one about those males of the species whose excess or deficiency in certain hormones leaves them like late 19th century rural Mayo homesteads after the Bailiff's visit?

***

The Baldy Song

(Air: 'Lid of me Granny's Bin')

There's societies for drug addictees, gamblers and alcoholics,
There's ones for those for those compelled to nick and dip in people's pockets,
Weight Watchers is for those who eat too much lard, spuds and bread,
But left out in the cold, alas, are men with baldy heads.

CHORUS:
For us it's wigs, transplants, slidin' roofs and glue,
Why can't we just relax and smile
Like hairy buggers do?

Have you ever seen an uncle wind the long stuff round his head
In neat, concentric, beehive rings—and clamp it down with gel?
That ruined hats and collars, scarves, the pillows and armchairs,
And you knew that all that greasy mess just stressed his lack of hair.
CHORUS

And did you ever notice those lads with JFK's face
Who look a bit like piebalds with a two-tone ridge and brace;
They have to grin forever to keep the thing in place.
Why don't they just get rid of it, accept their age with grace?
CHORUS

No self-respectin' State or board by-a baldy boy is led.
To the voters, full and coloured hair means trusty and well-led.
So wigs, implants, dyes and toupées screen executive marble heads
Like with Samson all a sign that they're strong, legal and well-bred.
CHORUS

Yet while you've admired poor Luke Kelly's scarlet, rugged, whinbush mop,
Spare a thought for Liam Clancy and his grafted snow-white cap;
With farmers, baseball players, chauffeurs, military and cops,
Self-image, power and self-esteem in under hats is locked .
CHORUS

But have you observed in music scenes the boys who pant and wheeze
With screwed up face and frozen lip a pulsing steady breeze, into
Saxophone and trumpet, oboe, whistle, flute and fife,
There's not the hair between them all to save a spider's life.
CHORUS

So take heart from Steven Berkoff, and Linford Christie's state,
Lenin's, Michael Gorbachev's and Kojak's shameless pates,
Brush Shiels, The Diceman, Matt Molloy, McCann and ould Yul Brenner,
And these days half the country's girls look like Sinéad O'Connor.
CHORUS

© *Fintan Vallely*

Martin O'Malley from Miltown Malbay in West Clare is an outstanding patron and enjoyer of traditional music and song. A farmer, the only thing which interferes with his hay-making is the cursed Willie Clancy Summer-School held in the first week of July, but which spills over to occupy the second. This is Ireland's university of the music and it attracts a vast entourage of musicians and maybe a thousand pupils annually. There was one sunny day reputedly in the wet summer of '85, and on it Martin was at the hay. He discarded all encumbrances to the process of rolling up the forkfuls and pitching and so on—i.e. heavy clothes—and set his teeth on the wall so that he could comfortably get stuck into the work. A jackdaw, however, took a fancy to the dentures and that was that. Two years later a neighbour found them (or was it them at all?) in a nest. The neighbour's name was, coincidentally, 'Crowe', so Martin coined the immortal words "robbed by a Jackdaw, brought back by a Crowe". These seemed a good foundation for a song. Miltown is hometown to the last reputed President of Ireland, and his bodyguards used to lounge around the front gate of the ancestral mansion when they weren't alleviating boredom by eating young cabbages or spinning idly around in Ford Granadas. They got some action eventually when the government organised a duck-hunt (Operation Mallard) which was inspired by a search for a mad dog out of which they eventually caught a fox.

The whole teeth escapade took place against the harangueings over the Anglo-Irish Agreement; *Dallas* was an American soap watched addictively in Ireland (it was reported that year that a migratory people in Africa postponed their annual up-and-away by two weeks to catch the last episode of the series); *Falcon Crest* is the Fine Gaelers' *Dallas,* and Crossmaglen is an area of South Armagh then heavily occupied by British troops. Garda Dillane used do a nixer at selling wood blocks: the Sergeant is a noted box player. Martin's form of transport was a black bike, and Sylvie (RIP) is the Friel's dog.

***

The Ballad of the Teeth

(Air: 'The Limerick Rake')

Nineteen eighty-five was a year of great angst
When Nic'rag-uans tried hard to keep out the Yanks,
When hay lay in August in mouldy wet hanks,
And the half of our farms were seized back by the banks.

From Dáil and Westminster we heard of harangues
About Ireland from people who don't give a dang,
About matters so personal and sacrosanct
As the bould Martin Malley's sad loss of his fangs.

This happened that one sunny day as he rolled
Up the cocks for his stock to keep out winter cold,
The sun scorched his fair skin and grilled his head gold
And before he realised he was out of control.

He threw down the rake and stretched out on a knoll
And fell asleep dreaming of ice-cream in bowls,
And of Shackleton's escapades to the South Pole
And locals in Greece under cool parasols.

Martin's molars shone bright in his wide-open maw
And attracted the eyes of a greedy jackdaw
Which plunged form the heavens, seized them in its claws,
And left Rip Van O'Malley with no way to chaw.

He woke two weeks later and to his dismay
His whole hay was lost, he had missed fourteen tays,
Two episodes of *Dallas* and two *Falcon Crest*
And a whole Willie season in Miltown Malbay.

Martin tore into town on his cabriolet,
And in Hillery's located the Gendarmerie
Who took fingerprints and compiled a dossier
Of suspects they knew to dip biscuits in tay.

From the woodcutter's cottage Dillane ably took charge
Of a massive task-force of all ranks of the Guards
Who abandoned their gateposts and Granada cars
To implement searching of *síbíns* and bars.

They scoured Miltown and Mullach late into the night
Until Sylvie in Friel's gave the sergeant a bite.
He called for his squeeze box, him foaming and white,
And composed a new tune he called Ray-bie's[50] delight.

Operation O'Mallard took off on the tear
Amid songs, jigs and reels, slides and polkas and airs
That were named after hens, chickens, pigeons and hares,
But for Martin's false teeth divil one of them cared.

Understandably Martin's lust wasn't the same
From mornin' to night he tramped boreens and lanes;
He terrorised thrushes and magpies and wrens
In the manner of soldiers around Crossmaglen.

But as seasons slipped by and without meat he dined,
He came to think he'd be worse off deaf or blind,
And to his new condition had come quite resigned
When glad tidings were brought in from out near Glendine.

For it seems that while robbin' birds' nests on his farm
A neighbour called Crowe gave a shout of alarm,
For leering at him among tinsel and coins
Was Martin's ould grin there all tangled in vines.

A fiesta was called to make up for his woe,
And Martin was interviewed on Gay Byrne's show:
With a glint in his eye he was not a bit slow—to say,
"Robbed by a jackdaw, brought back by a crow."

© *Fintan Vallely*

149

Whether it is the occasion of having to go to bed or to get up, the amount of it allowed at a pool game, in a swimming pool, or for having a tea break, the signal for the end of the night's crack or beginning of the day's work, 'Time' is always a seriously oppressive business. Sometimes people become agitated by it and unreasonably give out to the messengers—the bar staff, the timekeepers and so on; but there again they might go for the source of the trouble—the clock itself.

Mick Sullivan, from the lyric groves of West Cork, ended up doing this in the next song which is transported to these pages from the pen of George Curtin via the singing of Tim Lyons.

***

Mike Sullivan's Clock

This clock of Mick Sullivan's down in the bog,
It gave up keeping time when he started on grog;
It got into the habit of drinking strong wine
And it often struck eight when it should have struck nine.
Rally, fal, da, la, lah, rally fal, da, lah roh.

It often struck nine when it should have been eight
And it once struck twelve times when it wasn't so late;
It often broke out in the middle of the night
And kept hammering away till the clear morning light.
Rally, fal, da, la, lah, rally fal, da, lah roh.

Well, when it went to the divil, Micín took it down,
And he hitched up the pony to take it to town;
He wanted it fixed by a man from Tralee
But that very same day he was out on the spree.
Rally, fal, da, la, lah, rally fal, da, lah roh.

He then got it fixed by a smith from Pound Lane,
But when going home the ould clock went insane;
It struck everyone on the road that it met
And I'm told that it struck Mickel Arthurs to death.
Rally, fal, da, la, lah, rally fal, da, lah roh.

When Mick brought the clock back, he stood it up straight
And he oiled up the springs so the hammer would beat;
He dusted it out and adjusted the gong
And he tightened the screws with the paws of the tongs.
Rally, fal, da, la, lah, rally fal, da, lah roh.

He then hung it up on a sixpenny nail
And chastened its ardour with some kind of flail;
When I went to stop him, he warned me, "Watch out!"
He told me he'd break it without any doubt.
Rally, fal, da, la, lah, rally fal, da, lah roh.

He called down to Gerry and told him to run
And go and get Paddy to bring down the gun;
Paddy came down and he opened it out
And said it had got too much knocking about.
Rally, fal, da, la, lah, rally fal, da, lah roh.

Yerra, it stopped one fine day in the month of July
And those that saw it they couldn't say why;
From the nail on the wall sure it suddenly hopped
To the flag of the floor and 'twas there that it stopped.
Rally, fal, da, la, lah, rally fal, da, lah roh.

He went to the door and he shouted aloud
For to gather the neighbours or some sort of crowd,
And those that had weapons bring arms and sticks
And those that hadn't could break it with kicks.
Rally, fal, da, la, lah, rally fal, da, lah roh.

They all tore inside with pitchforks and clubs,
The houses were empty and so were the pubs;
Roaring and shouting with timber and rock
They soon put an end to Mick Sullivan's mad clock.
Rally, fal, da, la, lah, rally fal, da, lah roh.

The weather is always a good subject for a song, and traditionally as well as currently it is used in lyrics to set the scene and mood for human events being described. In Ireland we have 'weather', in Australia they don't. 'Weather' means a lack of sunshine, plenty of rain and cloud. The summer in Ireland begins generally in late June and ends in early July, so just imagine the kind of bad form there is if it begins late, or (and?) ends early. 1985 had such an alleged summer when one went diving for vegetables and trawled the fields for potatoes. The rain and the rain and the rain that year left us depressed for the next five (we finally came out of ourselves after we nearly bate England at the World Cup). The gloom was a national institution and was compounded by depressing radio broadcasters such as the somewhat inappropriately named Gay Byrne (a sort of Terry Wogan who never left, or a Phil Donahue whose great- grandparents didn't). Himself offered a start down under, he incited half the country to emigration by blethering on day after day about the joys of the greener hills over there in America and Australia. In the end he hadn't the nerve to go—leaving those foolish enough to believe in him now scratching their heads as they serve the real Americans their obscene dinners, clean their vast acreages of houses, wash their laundries of sweaty clothes and try to talk nicely to their boring, snotty children. That summer launched Tim Lyons into the style of song writing he'd always admired.

***

The Weather Song

Oh, it's rare I'm inspired or fired by poetic drive,
But conditions this year of Our Lord nineteen eighty-five
Have led me frustrated with hatred of this rain that we've had
To write down on paper this caper that's driving us mad.

Since the fifth of July the blue sky has never been seen;
There's all kinds of damps causing cramps, arthritis and spleen.
And farmers all day turning hay are being driven to stout;
They run into a bar for a jar, but they never come out.

And you read in the papers, bejapers, that nothing is right,
And to add to the fright, the potatoes have now got the blight.
The slugs and the snails have grown tails both hairy and long,
And they're eating each cabbage and turnip as they slide along.

And the expert in weather who nightly appears on the screen,
He points at the chart with his dart and his face turning green
As he forecasts low pressures and measures the strength of the gale,
Freak storm is the norm, forked lightning, loud thunder and hail.

And in Europe abroad, holy God! Alas and alack!
There's landslides and floods, an odd earthquake, it's all the same crack.
Snow blizzards abound around Bern in Switzerland high,
And all kinds of dogs, cats and mice descended from the sky.

And the people you meet in the street are sure to complain:
Emigrating, they shout: "We're going out to Morocco or Spain."
They're being driven away by the spray and the constant rainfall.
Even statues betimes in their shrines are being moved by it all.

So we'll drink up a glass and of summer-blue skies we will speak,
With mention of days when the haze of the sun made you weak.
Next year will be bright, sure the light will blind you for life,
And we'll forget that bad summer we suffered in nineteen eighty-five.

This song can be heard on the album Big Guns and Hairy Drums.

Anyone over forty who is of rural origin remembers 'the electric' arriving. For most of us who were children at the time, it was just another new thing, no more remarkable than the business of paraffin oil and candles. But it was considerably less interesting, because you couldn't hide from parental chastisement any more, you couldn't create a blowtorch wonder world by making holes in the lamp mantle, and you couldn't construct Dracula castles by implanting diversionary matchsticks in the candle wax. But for the older generation it was a sudden, ecstatic transition from squinting Aladdin, hurricane, Tilley and cart lamps (in whose gloomy ambience you could do nearly nothing after dark) to rooms bursting with light. For weeks after we got it in, my parents would be smiling from ear to ear every time they turned it on, and so precious was this new substance that it was not to be treated lightly—it was a privilege to pull the switch, and this was only done when it was totally justifiable and well after dusk. Some people marvelled so much that they had only the one bulb—in the kitchen. ("Sure aren't we only sleeping in the bedrooms anyway, what would we be doing with the light in there?" etc.)

Done methodically area by area, the coming of 'the electric' caused a great stir in the communities as it progressed. First the surveyors were out snooping around, grumpy and negotiating about where to put poles and transformers. Then the poles were dropped off—mysteriously, during the day while we were at school—the longest, straightest pieces of timber we had ever seen in our twisty sycamore and ash lands, all soaked in creosote. The young lads would gather round them, stamping, standing on them, trying to climb them, discussing this new wonder. Then the hole diggers and erectors were on the job. Nobody had ever seen anybody work so hard all at once, or wear such applied, all-weather, oiled clothing. The real dandies were the riggers and wire stringers—mysterious as pilots, climbing up into the sky like cats, winding and pulling, snipping off bits of bright copper wire, shouting and directing, getting the tension right. We fed and tea'd them like an army of liberation; we tore home from school each evening to get seeing what they'd done next. Heroes for the few days, these men were exciting, all powerful, and rare strangers in a country landscape; they came from faraway places like Randalstown or Templepatrick; they had mysterious accents and different stories. Our mothers loved the rare newness and the difference of faces and conversation. Our fathers puffed with pride for it gave them the scarce opportunity to be seen at work by outsiders, in charge, as masters of their demesnes, thrilled to meet someone to whom they could be generous. The 'electric men' were real frontiersmen who transformed people's lives and banished rural Ireland forever. Even the hardened, cynical natives of Coolea stood back in amazement in 1959 when the job was done there (a rare moment of weakness for an area where you can admit no weakness about anything to anyone for fear of having a satire penned about you). Séamus Mac Mathúna reports that one of the Lehanes, witnessing this community dropping of the guard, took the opportunity to drive home the vinegar pen.

***

When the ESB Came to Coolea

(Air: 'The Garden Where the Praties Grow', etc.)

Oh Johnny dear and did you hear what all the neighbours say?
For the ESB with 'lectricity is landed in Coolea.
For to give us light by day or night from lamps that do not blow
Out, dear oh dear, if we had them here, some fifty years ago.

We have Can Cullinane, a man of brawn, from Clonakilty town;
He climbs the poles with his iron soles, and he never yet fell down.
He can go so high up to the sky and watch the sputniks glow;
We had no sputniks in our sky some fifty years ago.

All the boys got jobs, they left the bogs and turf that would not dry;
For to dig the holes and stand the poles, they said they'd have a try.
For to draw the wire through bog and mire, sure 'tis a holy show;
Oh, Johnny dear, it would not do here, some fifty years ago.

We have Ned and Mack and Fuller Black, three engineers of fame;
In days gone by they sought so high to win that glorious name.
They could peg a line in the shortest time from Coome to Poulnabro;
We had no boys like these three guys some fifty years ago.

We have Major Dan, that crafty man, he drives a Bedford truck.
He comes at eight, sure he's never late to take the boys to work.
When he drives so smooth, they tap the hood, and they tell him to go slow.
His language then would shock old men some fifty years ago.

He's our foreman too, and 'twixt me and you, he's a right tough man.
They have to work just like a Turk (who told me was fat Dan).
For to dig the holes and stand the poles, with shovel, pick and crow,
Oh, Curley dear, you'd not do here some fifty years ago.

And our pay clerk Jer, we call him 'Sir', and he's a fine smart man;
'Tis our delight each Friday night when he drives up in his van,
With his smiling face and attaché case, pay packets filled with dough,
Oh, the bells would ring and sure we'd crown him king some fifty years ago.

Nothing looks more mundane than a Ford Transit van, it is to the settled community what the Hi-ace is to the Travellers. In all shapes, and with a supermarket choice of engine size, since it first came on the scene in the 1960s this vehicle was a revolution—and it is still going around. We would never have got as far as we have without it. They were turned into minibuses and ambulances, breakdown trucks, mobile homes, mobile bombs and mortar launch pads—even in Whitehall. Without it we would never have had crime, law, social breakdown, music, hippies, smuggling, theatre, building, ice-cream or a living Pope. And then Toyota had to come along and ruin it all. This is the epitaph for the Transit's heyday.

***

The Transit Van

Margaret Thatcher on TV looked so sincere as she says to me,
"There'd be no unemployment if yis'd all use a bit of initiative."
I was on the dole, I was broke and bored,
Says I, "I'll take her at her word."
So I talked to the Credit Union[51] man, and bought meself a Transit van.

For me next step up the ladder now, I bought meself an ould fat sow.
I crossed the Border quite legally, and collected the EC subsidy,
Signed all the forms, handed back the pen,
Then smuggled me sow back home again.
Ten times a day we'd work this plan—meself, the sow and the Transit van.

Of travel-sickness this sow pig died. Says I, "It's time to diversify."
I took all me money from the biscuit tin, filled the van to the roof
    with whiskey and gin,
And around the south my wares I'd sell
In public houses and hotels.
There was never a guard or a Customs man got their nose inside that transit van.

At festivals and Fleadhs and fairs, if the crack was good you'd find me there,
At all big matches in Croke Park, even dancin' at Springsteen in the dark;
I've fought with tinkers in Ballinasloe,
I've danced on the streets around Listowel;
Mothers had their daughters warned, stay well away from that Transit van.

It bein' Lent and the drink trade slow, I changed to carryin' videos,
While on the road to Ballybay, found a Customs roadblock on me way;
To face the border I got it turned,
The engine roared and the tyres burned
And five patrol cars fully manned were in hot pursuit of the Transit van.

Through Clontibret I did run as quick as Peter Robinson,
Goin' round a corner I hit a dog, went over the hedge in the Gallow Bog.
I sat on the bank watchin' all I owned
Sinkin' in a boghole like a stone.
It was lyin on its back and the wheels still turnin' with the stereo playin'
        'Farewell to Erin'.

Now I'm back where I first began, no job, no money, but I've a plan:
There's a wee girl down in Tullysarn, she could hould my future in her hand.
Now she doesn't look like a film star,
But she's been tellin me about her da:
He owns no property nor land—but he has two sows and a Transit van.

For the Queen of England drives a Rolls Royce car,
Her son Charlie has a Jaguar,
But when the Pope came to Ireland,
He drove about in a Transit van.

© Sean Mone

159

Part 13: Media Mundanity

Strange things happen in Ireland. There are strange people who speak an unintelligible dialect which is designed so that no-one—not even the speaker—can understand it. It is most successfully passed from father to son, although there are exceptional circumstances in which a wife or daughter might acquire it, but only if the father or brother dies. On occasions even those who do actually speak it become so confused by other speakers that they are obliged to fall back on the aid of simultaneous translation devices. These people are politicians, and the dialect they think they are communicating with is best described by the term coined by the Irish Liberal Conor Cruise O'Brien—'GUBU'. He is an acknowledged expert in it himself. GUBU is an abbreviation for "Grotesque, unbelievable, bizarre and unprecedented"—the words uttered by CJ Haughey when he discovered that his Attorney General, Patrick Connolly, was inadvertently hosting an unsavoury, but impeccably upper-class, arrogant character called Malcolm MacArthur who, while pursuing effort-free wealth during the summer of 1982, had done in a farmer for a shotgun and a nurse for her car. Mickey McConnell, for years a journalist in *The Irish Times,* finally got so sick of translating 'GUBU' into plain talk (called 'sub-editing') that he gave up the job, and wrote his career an epitaph. It expresses his dazzling grasp of the tongue in an honest appraisal of his life up to the point where he escaped to live in bliss in Kerry.

The GUBU Song

For twenty frantic, fruitless years I've worked in Dublin town,
Reporting for newspapers, I was busy writing down
All the words of politicians in my endless quest for truth:
It was such a wasted exercise, I squandered all my youth.
That's the cause of my condition now, as I'll explain to you,
For I find myself now talking like the politicians do.
So if somebody asks 'do I take sugar in me tay'—
I freeze, put on a plastic smile, and this is what I say:

CHORUS:
"Well, I'm very glad you asked me that, for at this point in time,
In the circumstances that prevail there is in the pipeline
Infrastructural implications interfaced with lines of thought
Which lead to grassroots viabilities, which at this point I'd rather not
Enunciate in ambiguities, but rather seek to find
Negotiated compromises which is the bottom line
For full and frank discussions which could serve to integrate
With basic fundamental principles to which we all relate
And not indoctrinaire philosophies which any fool can see
In inescapable hypotheses confronting you and me,
But in the interests of the common good, now you need never fear—
And I'm very glad yo asked me that, I'm glad I made things clear.

Now, as you can imagine, this has greatly changed my life.
An example was the fateful day on which I wed my wife.
All went well until the moment that the priest said with a smile,
"Do you take this woman for your wife?"—I winced as I replied:
CHORUS

And now I'm lyin' on me deathbed and I'm full of mortal dread,
For I know that almost certainly I'll very soon be dead.
And when Saint Peter asks me, "Do you want to come on in?"
I'm sure to face damnation—for I know I'll say to him:
CHORUS

© Micky McConnell

161

At the end of 1983 Ireland was embroiled in a kidnap drama. TV had a field-day on something the paranoic scale of *Sky News* and the latest Middle East, media-mediated crises today, and we tuned in as many times as possible to hear the hysterical, the sombre, the profound, the analytical, the emotional and the simple raving. Don Tidey had been held to ransom by the IRA for his supermarket millions and the whole thing was good licence value. We were bitterly deprived of diversion when it ended suddenly with a dramatic incident in Ballinamore, Co. Leitrim, in which a soldier and a Garda were killed. Who shot who was never clear. *Today Tonight*, a current affairs magazine programme, sent a reporter, Brendan O'Brien, up to Ballinamore to investigate how the locals could possibly have kept silent about the presence of a kidnap victim in the area while the rest of the country was being ransacked looking for him. The local peasantry wouldn't co-operate, however, offering him only "No comm-ent". Brendan was incredulous—these people were refusing to talk to their national media. A comment was eventually solicited from some strap of a twelve-year old male, but even that child was adamant that he would keep such a secret: "No comm-ent". Never was the difference between city Ireland and rural Ireland so underlined. The Gardai were only able to supply the starving press with little other than a detailed inventory of the 'kitchen' of the hole in the ground where Mr Tidey had been held captive. The piece is a parody on the late Peadar (senior) Mac Giolla Cearr's 'Man from the *Daily Mail*' which sent up British Press hysteria about Ireland in the early 1920s. It was sung by Christy Moore from here to California and Australia, recorded by him too but considered worthless by him and so was properly given away for nothing—in the company of John Maguire's 'Hey Ronnie Reagan' song—on a single attached to the *Ride On* album…

***

Leitrim is a Very Funny Place

(Air: 'The Darlin Girl from Clare', 'The Man from the Daily Mail', etc.)

Leitrim is a very funny place, Sir.
It's a strange and distant land.
All the boys there are in the IRA, Sir,
All the girls in Cumann na mBan.

Every tractor has a Nicky Kelly[52] sticker.
Nobody will talk to me.
Ah, you know it was no wonder
That the Guards made a blunder,
Said the man from RTÉ

CHORUS:
Every bird, upon my word
Is singin' treble, "I'm a rebel."
Every hen, indeed, is layin' hand-grenades
Up there, Sir, in Dromahair, Sir,
And every cock in the Kinloch stock
Says it's longin' to be free.
Sheep and lambs are advisin'
That there be another risin',
Says the man from RTÉ.

Today Tonight I went to Ballinamore, Sir.
I was briefed by the Gardaí.
On a video they showed me Provos
Eatin' curry and drinkin' tea.
They were all wearin' Russian balaclavas,
Each carried an RPG,[53]
British scalps around their tummies,
Pockets full of stolen money,
Says the man from RTÉ.
CHORUS

This whole place is seethin' with sedition,
It's Sinn Féin through and through.
All the Task Force have joined the local Unit,
The Post Office is the GHQ.[54]
There's a racetrack underground for keepin' Shergar[55]
"No comm-ent!" is all they'll say to me.
Subversion here is bubblin',
Oh! Please take me back to Dublin!
Says the man from RTÉ.

© Fintan Vallely. The song has also appeared in Frank Connolly's The Christy Moore Songbook, and Christy Moore's own One Voice - My Life in Song.

The first flake of snow is a welcome sight to any beleaguered broadcaster. We get so little of it that it's a big deal, and commands all sorts of analysis, way beyond the complexity of its microscopic crystalline complexity. So when it begins to fall, the DJ's, chat show hosts, and political gurus even, lift the wee red hatchet, break the glass, get the key and open the Pandora's box of woe and warning that is marked SNOW.

"Do not leave your homes" is not an uncommon piece of advice. But hysteria reigned back in the 'big snows' of the 1970s and 80s expected them, they crept up on us and caught us by surprise and we weren't prepared. Even the weather people got the shock of their lives. So fraught did things get that otherwise ice-cool dudes like RTÉ presenter Derek Davis lost their reason and went bald-headed for the Met office people who were, for a change, summoned into the Studio and asked to account for their behaviour. But, while snow was the instigation of this song, nevertheless, like radio announcers, it took on a power and a personality all of its own. At this point it's very much a lament at the passing of RTÉ's monopoly of the airwaves with its clichéd defensiveness—the result of years and years of job-immobility suffered by its otherwise-very-well-looked-after Public Service employees. Nowadays of course radio is indescribable for the incontinence of its mawkishness, self pity, self deprecation, whining and yapping, all heeled out over us in a slop of consumer-centred talk-shows which render the confession box, the court of law, common sense and basic human dignity irrelevant.

***

The Studio Song

(Air: 'Pick Me Up on Your Way Down')

Babies, airports, Provo moles,
TV spongers, farmer's dole,
Tax-dodgers, Charlie Haughey,
Pirate Stations, poor Sean Doherty,
The grotesque and unbelievable,
Bizarre and inconceivable,
For you are all achievable,
Thanks to my studio.

CHORUS:
Lock me up, O, O, O Lock me up,
O, O, O Lock me in my studio.
Save me from the snowflakes,
Plastic bullets, drugs and buckrakes, O, O,
Lock me in my studio.

Earthquakes, floods and hurricanes,
Oil-slicks and Dáil change,
General panic, fires, wrecked trains,
Fox and mallard hunts, crashed planes,
Yes at times I sound insane
And my pathos seems deranged,
But responsibility's a strain
Here in my studio.
CHORUS

Holy pictures, and bells toll—ing,
Underscore my sacred rôle;
I'm the Nation's voice and soul,
Moralistic bright and bold.
Lock your doors, alarm your cars,
Drink at home, don't drive to bars
And remember! When it snows,
contact my studio.

© *Fintan Vallely*

Television advertisements can be annoying at times. Especially when they plagiarise a good tune, leaving it unfit to be ever played by human hand again. Particularly so victimised has been the work of the 16/17th composer Turloch Carolan who is now best known in connection with flitches of bacon, silos of fermenting barley and lumps of cheese. So too at the 1995 Cork Folk Festival, where in the middle of the Malagasy group Tarika's show an excited punter was shouting "Nescafe!"—á la a then-current TV coffee ad which was set in Colombia (but to that particular set of Cork ears anywhere far away might have done). While no-one has yet utilised the Famine in a potato advert, Benetton are thought to be working on it...

Déaglán Tallon's talents at the verbal arts were legend. A frustrated hedge schoolmaster himself, he missed his vocation by as little as a century. Content he became however to take his ease among the rhododendroned glades of West Cork, where Argentinean honey-bees imperially pillage the local nectar. There, too, some of the good natives wreak constant revenge on their former persecutors by manufacturing toy British soldiers[56] which by virtue of their robust construction will still be being tortured by Irish children well into the 22nd century. Déaglán personally took great delight in slandering the sacred institutions of consumerism as well as some of his best friends. Small wonder that because of the Del Monte advert he ended up hating pineapples.

***

The Man from Del Monte

And the Man from Del Monte smiled and said,
"You can have them sliced or you can have them whole
And either way my pineapples are pure gold."
And the Man from the Ministry said you're welcome to the fold
And you'll pay no taxes and get your grants just like it's told."
And the Man from the Media wrote in capitals bold
Being grateful for the advertisement he'd just sold
That these pineapples must surely be solid gold.
And the Man from the Mountain said the Man from Del Monte
Could stick his pineapple up his hole.

And the Man from Del Monte smiled sweetly at the twit
And said his great-grandmother was Irish and a wit,
And anyway the Emerald Isle really was his thing.
And the Man from the Ministry said with a grin
Pay no heed to the eegit and called for more gin,
And the Man from the Media penned an erudite panegyric
Praising the benefits of progress and of foreign companies coming in.
And the Man from the Mountain said the Man from Del Monte
Should shove his pineapple up where
The Kerryman hid his threepenny bit.

And the Man from Del Monte smiled and counted his cash
And said to the Man from the Ministry, "Thanks,
Thanks for the million and also for the factory
With the view of the mountain where the pineapples grow."
And the Man from the Ministry said, "You're welcome, pal,
And thank you for the jobs and also for the kick-back."
And the Man from the Media wrote that 'twas all very grand
And that anyone who rocked the boat was a confounded ass.
And the Man from the Mountain said the Man from Del Monte
Could shove his factory and his pineapple up
The highest rafter of his arse.

And the Man from Del Monte smiled though rather sore,
And said this sort of thing drove capital from our shore
And the Man from the Ministry was grim and by four
That afternoon had spoken to a friend of a friend who swore
That it wouldn't be a problem and he'd get it under control.
And the Man from the Media screamed and raised a furore
About ungrateful peasants who created such an unholy show;
And the Man from the Mountain spoke—no more.

© *Déaglán Tallon*

Part 14: Murder Most Foul

A nybody who hasn't been to secondary school might skip this lyric. Anybody who has, can wonder at its finely-crafted excellence and gasp with astonishment at how its author, Adam McNaughton from Glasgow, has actually managed the impossible. The poet was determined that no other bastard was going to sing it but him. Firstly he wrote it in Scots, the language, of course, of the play's characters, and which limits the number of chancers singing it in pubs to Scottish ones, thus ruling out a 'Willie Mac Bride' fate. Secondly, if you can pass through that coarse sieve, an even finer mesh confronts you: the air is 'The Mason's Apron'. The mere three-part version is a concession the poet grudgingly makes.

***

Oor Hamlet

(Air: 'The Mason's Apron')

There was this king sittin' in his gairden all a-lane
When his brither in his ear poured a wee taste o' henbane,
Then he stole his brither's crown an' his money an' his widda,
But the deid king walked an' gat his son an' said "Hey, listen kiddo:

Ah've been kilt an' it's your du-ty to take revenge on Claudius—
Kill him quick an' clean an' show the nation what a fraud he is."
The boy says "Right, ah'll dae it, but ah'll need to play it crafty—
So that naeb'dy will suspect me—ah'll kid on that Ah'm a daftie".

So wi' a' excep' Horatio—(An' he trusts him as a friend)
Hamlet (that's the boay) kids on he's roon the bend,
An' because he wisnae ready for obligatory killin'
He tried to make the king think he was tuppence aff the shillin'.
    Took the mickey oot Polonius—treatit poor Ophelia vile,
    Tellt Rosencrantz and Guildenstern that Denmark was a jile,
    Then a troupe o' travellin' actors like the 7.84
    Arrived to dae a special wan-night gig in Elsinore.

CHORUS:
Hamlet, Hamlet, loved his maa-my, Hamlet, Hamlet, actin' ba'my,
Hamlet, Hamlet, hesitatin', wonders if the ghost's a cheat
An' that is how he's waitin'.

Then Hamlet wrote a scene for the players to enact
While Horatio an' him wad watch to see if Claudius cracked
The play was called 'The Moosetrap' (no the wan that's runnin' noo),
An' sure enough the king walked out afore the scene was through.
    So Hamlet's got the proof that Claudius gi'ed his dad the dose,
    The only problem bein' noo that Claudius knows he knows.
    So while Hamlet tells his ma that her new husband's no a fit wan,
    Uncle Claude pits oot a contract wi' the English king as hit-man.

Then when Hamlet kilt Polonius the concealed *corpus delecti*
Was the king's excuse to send him for an English hempen neck-tie
Wi' Rosencrantz an' Guildenstern to make sure that he goat there,
But Hamlet jumped the boat an' pit the finger oan that pair.
    Meanwhile Laertes heard his da'ad been stabbed through the arras,
    He came racin' back to Elsinore *toot-suite* hotfoot frae Paris,
    An' Ophelia wi' her da kilt by the man she wished to marry—
    Eiftir sayin' it wi' flooers she committed *hari-kari*.

Hamlet, Hamlet, loved his maa-my, Hamlet, Hamlet, actin' ba'my
Hamlet, Hamlet, Hesitatin', wonders if the ghost's a cheat
An' that is how he's waitin'.

Then Laertes lost the place an' was demandin' retribution, an' the
King says, "Keep the heid an' Ah'll provide ye a solution."
He arranged a sword fight for the interestit pairties
Wi' a bluntit sword for Hamlet an' a sharp one for Laertes.
    An' to make things double sure (the auld 'belt an braces' line)
    He fixed a poisont sword-tip an' a poisont cup o' wine.
    The poisont sword got Hamlet but Laertes went an' muffed it—
    'Cauuse he goat stabbed hissel an' he confessed afore he snuffed it.

Hamlet's nanny drank the wine, a-an' as her face turnt blue
Hamlet says, "Ah quite believe the king's a baddie noo."
"Incestuous, treacherous, dam-med Dane," he said (to be precise),
An' made up for hesitatin' by killin' Claudius twice,
    'Cause he stabbed him wi' the sword an' forced the wine atween his lips,
    Then he cried, "The rest is silence!"—that was Hamlet had his chips.
    They fired a volley ow-er him that shook the topmaist rafter,
    An' Fortinbras, knee-deep in Danes, lived happy ever after.

Hamlet, Hamlet, a' the gory, Hamlet, Hamlet, Ah'm away!
If you think this is borin'—you should read the bloody play!

© Adam McNaughton

The road to the traditional ballad-lover's heart is littered with the corpses of victims of cold-hearted murders, political slayings, love's suicide pacts and maidens done in by bastards who pretended in court that they were only shooting swans. Superficial forensic observation reveals that death has been caused by a variety of applied instruments—daggers, musket-balls, poison, fingers, stones, dynamite, ropes and plenty of water. This territory is the main dish for the serious song connoisseur; the other stuff is only a snack. Sometime after the Traditional music renaissance began in Ireland of the 70s, unknownst to its followers it became commoditised. Behind the enterprise was the inevitable force of the entrepreneurial spirit, that crusading force which leads us all to hate everything, yet without which we couldn't get anything done. Here it took the form of the gombeen men ("ancestral yuppies" as singer Sean Garvey calls them), the lads who had been thinking in stereo long before Phillips had ever dreamt of it. They knew how to make the few bob out of Traditional music, and keep the flag of things national, important and worthy flying at the same time.

The concept of the grocer-cum-publican is a common enough thing in rural anywhere, and sometimes the franchise for the Post Office (carrying its bonus of Social Welfare and Pension payments, all of which came to be spent in the emporium) might share the location too. Joe Frawley, like many's the good ladder-climber before him, augmented the power of the man behind the bar with dabbling in the political barrel, often the rock upon which great parties are founded. The pub, of course, in any remote area is also the Leisure Centre, and although you can't take part in vigorous activities, other than lip wrestling, bladder expansion and contraction, penis-shaking, hand-washing and toilet flushing, you can take part in all sorts of low-energy sports which present no crisis to the sebaceous glands. These are organised, generously, by the Boss. In addition, Irish women have now taken to the pub in a big way, having become pissed off with staying at home. This was, of course, as elsewhere noted, encouraged by the epidemic of addiction to *Dallas* and Joan Collins, not to mention the filtered ideologies of Simone de Beauvoir and Betty Friedan, or the flush of droll commentating by Nell McCafferty. The female presence has had the effect of encouraging the cleaning-up of some of the filthier lounges, the unblocking of pissoirs, the provision of toilet brushes and rolls, soap and sandwiches, the installation of carpets, armchairs and couches, television sets and sometimes traffic lights—not to mention of course the suspension of mysterious multifaceted rotating mirrorballs from high ceilings. And music too is provided to cope for the thinking species, sometimes the native sort, but often in a cocktail with Country and Popular balladry. To save on the enormous overheads, the local Traditional musicians may be lured in by slabbering about 'Tradition', calling a *seisiúin*, and spreading the rumour of a free pint. This is most easily organised through the non-tea-drinking strata of Comhaltas Ceoltoiri Éireann, the people who organise the Fleadhnna Cheoil and who have branches in every haggard. Here Tim Lyons has a go at both the gombeen man and the traditional murder ballad, and so he murders the genre and the genre murders the publican—without whom and whose premises it cannot of course survive.

***

The Grisly Murder of Joe Frawley

(Air: 'The Flower of Sweet Strabane')

I'll sing of Mike-ey Cleary who in this town did dwell;
He worked in Frawley's music lounge, a-a place you all know well.
Joe Frawley was a councillor, full of wit and rural charm,
With a Mace Food Store in the shop next door—and a ninety acre farm.

When the week it starts he has cards and darts,
On Tuesdays there's nothing much;
On Wednesdays there's a disco bar
With flashing lights and such.
The local Comhaltas meeting
Goes wild on Thursday nights,
But it's when the weekend comes around—
Man, it's really out of sight.

For from bogs and drains,
From shady lanes,
From the woodwork everywhere,
On buckrakes and in motoring cars
They do assemble there
With tin whistles and with mandolins

172

And bouzoukis by the score,
Bodhráns, and bones,
Mouth organs, spoons
And the Portuguese guitar.

I'll also sing of Brídhgín Ring,
Out the country she did live.
She fell in love with young Cleary
For the service he could give.
For 'twas many's the toasted sandwich
He-e slipped free across the bar,
And many's the *West Coast Cooler* too—
In fact lashings of free jar.

But word did spill, as word soon will,
Where there's complimentary beer.
A local spy who lived nearby
Whispered in Joe Frawley's ear:
"Your profits are going down the tubes
With Cleary pulling your pints—
They're being given away, for SFA,
To the young-one smoking joints."

A-a-and when he heard these dreadful words
His face turned a greenish grey;
Unto his lovesick ba-ar man
These awful words did say:
"You will repay without delay
All the money that you stole
Or it's lose the job without a bob
And I'll bar you from the Dole."

From shady lanes, from bogs and drains,
From the woodwork everywhere
In buckrakes and in motoring cars
They do assemble there;
With fiddles there and ban-joes too,
Paolo Sopranis small and large,
Mandocellos, flutes, Celtic harps and lutes
And a flat-bellied, twelve-string blarge.

This happened all on a wet weekend
Five days before the Fleadh.
She'd gone up to her father
Saying u-un to him, "Da,
I'm thumbing into town a while
To see what I can see
To down the black, and have some crack,
And hear some Schitheredee."

A-a-and when she walk-ed in the pub
She was ready all for the booze.
Ould Frawley came right up to her
And his words did careful choose.
It was at this fair young maiden
He then threw the bloody book, saying
"You won't get tight in here this night—
So FUCK OFF AND SLING YOUR HOOK."

And when she heard these boring words
She shed not a single tear,
But swore by all the burning bras
From here to Germaine Greer
That she would get revenge on him
And slit his slimy throat
And throw his body all in the lake
And spoil her Fine Gael vote.

From bogs and drains, from shady lanes,
From the woodwork everywhere,
In buckrakes and in motoring cars
They do assemble there;
With concertinas rare from County Clare,
Hurdi gurdis on the ran by the ton,
And continental types
With Uilleann pipes,
Bombards and snare drums.

So-o as he was making silage
On th'ould swamp that he called his farm,
It was quite true he had no clue
That he would come to harm;
For she crept up close behind him
With a *Black Diamond* banjo wire,
And she strung it tight round his wind-pipe
And fecked him all in the mire.

Whe-en the Gardaí heard of this
Their statement it was quite clear:
"We have reasonable suspicion
Foul play was in-volved here,
For we found his carcass floating
On the bottom of the lake
And those marks around his windpipe
A blunt instrument did make."

And when she was accused of it
Her solicitor he did say:
"My client pleads 'Not Guilty'
Unto her dying day."
But the judge he roared, "NOT LIKELY!",
And his mouth obscured by foam:
"It's round the bend your life you'll spend
In a psy-chi-at-ric home."

Ould Frawley he was buried,
In a coffin, a cask or bier,
And the ghost of crazy Brídhgín
Whispered in his tone-deaf ear:
"I've stilled your life for-ever
You chau-vin-is-tic little shower—
You'll be calling 'TIME!' for ever more
Where there's never a holy hour."

© *Tim Lyons*

Part 15: Parish Pumpery

THE SHADES OF ASHGROVE

Beauty is in the eye of the beholder. *An Bord Fáilte*, the one-time Irish Tourist Board, spent a fortune telling the outsider what is beautiful, but most people, especially local hotel and pub owners, know only too well the fantastic charms of their own spot. And so there isn't a boghole in the country that hasn't got a song written in praise of it. This vast numbers of songs glorifying writers' favoured bowers prompts that generous, gushing fountain of throwaway wit—song collector, bard and hands-on academic, the late, much lamented Dr. Tom Munnelly—to suggest that "all Clare songs are written by travel agents". He might have remarked that the effusions of the 19th century Darby Ryan sound as if they were written by a florist. Ryan, author of *The Peeler and the Goat*, began life as Diarmuid Ó Ríain, son of well-to-do farmers, around 1777 at Ashgrove, near Bansha, on the brink of the song-famed Glen of Aherlow in Co. Tipperary. He died in 1855, leaving his song as an immortal memorial. An eye-witness account of the bard is handed down by a descendant[57] Sean Ó Grúagáin:

"I knew only one person who remembered seeing Darby Ryan. He was Dónal O'Ríain of Rossadrehid, a relative of the poet and the last Irish speaker in the Glen. Dónal, who died in 1910, described the poet as being well over medium height, healthy and robust. His dress was typical of the time—frieze coat, corduroy kneebreeches

176

and gilt buttons, sheep's-grey stockings, semi-Billy Gladstone collar and tie. Of course he wore the ordinary *báinín* when working—one spun by the local weaver, Pat Fitzgerald, who died about 1894."

Educated in the hedge-school—which may account for his romantic birl—Darby was an avid reader who plundered the contemporary and incunabular literary resources of his betters in development of his intellectual needs. An early attempt to turn him into a priest—on account of his way with words—fortunately failed (or we would never have heard any more about him), the death of a brother forcing him back to a life of farm drudgery. This had the benefit of involving him in the land agitation of the times, which in turn catalysed his literary political output, some of which was in Irish. His most dramatic piece, 'Ireland's Lament' survives printed in *The Tipperary Minstrel,* to be found, like everything else, in The British Museum. Darby wrote many flowery recitations which demonstrate the search for expression through Hiberno-English—literal use of the cumbersome English language by one who was acquainted with lyric style in Irish. He incorporates the minutest detail, making one wonder was he trying to educate, as well as impress, his listeners with his knowledge. One of his songs lampoons a tailor for making a hames[58] out of his new suit, but in the process it details all the processes and implements used. The song which follows has passionate dignity and self-confidence oozing from its every line, perhaps symptomatic of the development of the National movement in the years after the 1801 Act of Union, leading up to Catholic Emancipation in 1829 which gave political—and, in the process, cultural—recognition and thus identity and self-reliance to the Catholic Irish.

***

The Shades of Ashgrove

(Air: 'The Banks of Sullane')

You bright Helliconian maidens, your favours I humbly implore,
Vouschafe to assist my endeavours in eloquent measures to soar
My talents in truth are unequal, unless I'm inspired from Above,
To set forth in suitable phrases the beauties of verdant Ashgrove.

Its valleys are fanned by the zephyrs, by gentle and temperate breeze;
The honey, in quick distillation, drips down from the fruit-bearing trees.
The prolific mares they are grazing, and cattle, full many a drove;
The lambkins are wantonly playing and straying by the Shades of Ashgrove.

The Aherlow's clear, crystal current, as nectar, transparent and pure
Glides gently in tardy meander, reluctantly joining the Suir;
Like the Nile's fertile inundations, the adjacent fair meadows improve,
Ensuring nature's rich vegetation along the sweet shades of Ashgrove.

Gay flora with exquisite favour on her fields in all seasons bestows:
The violet, the lily and daisy, the tulip, carnation and rose;
Here all sorts of flowers grow spontaneous, in each sunny vale and alcove,
In abundance without cultivation, along the sweet Shades of Ashgrove.

No pestilence, death or contagion ere haunted this fertilised place.
The healthy and contented natives enjoy a full measure of peace.
When Adam was banished from Eden, in desolate regions to rove,
He preferred before all other places to dwell by the Shades of Ashgrove.

'Tis now I am come to a finish, kind neighbours, I bid you adieu.
Exempt from all exaggeration, I give to my birthplace its due.
If critics should scoff I'm quite heedless, whether they disprove or approve,
Come, toast off in copious libations, success to the Shades of Ashgrove.

© Darby Ryan, c. 1830

Other midsummer idyllicisms are usually modelled on such a grand, classical structure, but sometimes the great local beauty is described all the more vividly by its superior comparison with the wonders of the world. Patsy Cronin from Toureen, Kilgarvan, Co. Kerry, with his brother Mick played music on fiddles they made themselves. Patsy was not a great traveller—the longest he was ever away from home was a night they spent interned in Ballyvourney Hall after being arrested by Black and Tans (he never again set foot in Ballyvourney). But Patsy knew the world intimately, for he was an avid reader of newspapers, atlases and books which were supplemented by verbal travel accounts of the colonies and wars. All of this he acquired from English visitors who came shooting grouse on the local mountain. Ever ready for new ideas, once, when given an early book on Lourdes the brothers built a grotto on a stream at the end of the house, thereby creating a fashion which is still with us (no wonder the statues chose the South West to start their movement). This, and his songs, show that he anticipated the development of 'virtual reality' by at least seventy years. Always a versifier, once when the brothers were expecting the vet, but had to go cutting turf, Patsy dictated a note for Micky to write:

> The Cronin boys to the bogs have gone,
> On the banks of turf you'll find them
> With their sleáns and their pikes, and their two clay pipes
> And their shirts hanging out behind them.

After the brothers' deaths in the early 60s, the heir spent two weeks burning their books and papers; the house ended up a derelict ruin in the middle of a State forest. All that survived were a notebook of songs (now, usefully, in a library in the USA) and a letter to the Pope (sent via Cardinal Logue, but never replied to—or was it ever forwarded?)[59]. They (the Cronins) had been excommunicated for membership of the post-Treaty IRA and were making an appeal to the Roman gentleman that this must be invalid since the Catholic Church was thereby taking sides in a political struggle. In both Patsy Cronin's songs and encyclical he shows no shortage of imagination, and were he still alive he would have no hope of ever getting on *The Late Late Show*. Patsy's self-composed epitaph says it all:

Here lies the body of poor old Pat.
He looked like a fool but he was not:
Amateur author, sculptor, pauper,
Master craftsman, What!

The final stanza to his 'Beauty Spot Glanlea' was composed in more recent years by his fan club in the Top of Coome pub on the West Cork/Kerry mountainy border who utilise subversive liquids to achieve ever greater altitudes in hallucinogenic, lyrical hang-gliding, and who still sing the song verse by verse 'round the house'.

***

Beauty Spot Glanlea

Come all ye wanderin' travellers, of every rank and station,
And hear my short narration which has yet remained untold,
And though you be an African, a German or a Bulgarian,
Regardless of such variance the truth I will unfold.
You'll hear of great dis-unity unveiled to the community,
So take this opportunity to listen here to me;
And you'll hear of many foreign lands and truthful calculations
And of my few relations round my home in Sweet Glan-lea.

I went to see the world's rage though scarcely sixteen years of age,
A steerage passage I engaged on a ship called 'Iron Duke'.
We went on board at Dublin's Wall bein' southward bound for the Transvaal.
I had a friend from Annascaul and one from Donnybrook.
Our noble ship had scarcely steamed when into mind fond memories gleamed,
I thought on my dear neighbours and their loving company.
And I thought of my dear brothers and our love for one another
And of a gentle mother there at home in sweet Glanlea.

We landed safe and suddenly in that British State Cape Colony,
In search of manual labour I wandered near and far.
I searched the Orange River amongst Hottentots and Caphirs
Till I found work at some caper on the Isle of Zanzibar.

A Dutchman who admired my ways took me to see the Himalayas
Oh, oh boys indeed I was amazed their awful heights to see.
And we journeyed on through Hindustan and up the river Gan-ges, but
No place in all those ran-ges was like home in sweet Glanlea.

Now this Dutchman who in health declined had heard of cures in Palestine
And persuaded me for to combine and along with him to go.
We landed safe in Jaffa and we journeyed to Jerusalem,
The ancient city of Hebron and the ruins of Jericho.
   The Le-bán-on mountains' highest peaks were like McGillicuddy's reeks
   And from their summits you could see the lake of Galilee.
   And likewise the river Jordan, and the province of Samaria, and
   Though it sounds contrary—Ah!! the fairest was Glanlea.

But a doleful time soon drifted nigh when this faithful Dutchman friend and I
Were about to part and bid good-bye, perhaps to meet no more.
I stood forlorn upon the quay as the ship that bore him sailed away.
His memory in my heart will stay till life's long reign is o'er.
   In Palestine I met all kinds and read of San Francisco's mines—
   There for to invest my capital I thought a good idea.
   Oh but oft mid speculation I would pause for recreation
   And go home in contemplation to my home in sweet Glanlea.

So providence thus gone my way and therefore conscience I obeyed;
I took a ship and sailed away as my friends did me forsake
I arrived in San Francisco where the trees were blooming beautiful,
But on that self-same evening there was a big earthquake.
   I was in bed and sleeping sound when I woke to find things
      tumbling round
   And after that there was no sound, no pain afflicted me.
   And on the following morning when I recovered consciousness
   I wrote of all the consequence to my home in sweet Glanlea.

I told them in my letter how I'd lost the situation
That was all my worldly station, and I intended to go home.
And I hoped their generosity would aid my transportation
And I went on relating how misfortune made me roam.
    I got some cash to pay my way without disaster or delay
    And soon arrived in Queenstown Quay on board a chimpanzee.
    And after an excursion of a few short hours duration
    I reached that little station on the road to sweet Glanlea.

But as I approached the terminus I viewed with consternation
A mighty congregation all assembled in the rain.
Sure I thought some other person of great worldly estimation
To their eager expectation was arriving home by train.
    But as I scanned each smiling face, t'was all friends and neighbours,
        old time mates,
    Had gathered there in hundreds with a welcome home for me.
    And they shouted with elation till they shook with great vibration
    The surrounding elevations on the road to sweet Glanlea.

And now I live contentedly amongst those grand ould neighbours
Endowed with every caper of good nature and delight.
Where enraptured by flirtation with a lover, soon temptation
And mutual admiration joined me here with her for life.
    And now we meet each Sunday noon in that cosy spot called
        Top of Coome
    Where the songs and stories would illume the hearts of you and me.
    And it's there amongst the multitude in quietness, peace and pulchritude
    I tireless pour beatitudes upon you, sweet Glanlea.

The full song sung 'round the house' is on the superb RTÉ DVD Come West Along the Road 2 sung definitively by Danny Kelleher, & Diarmaid, Eoiní Maidhcí & Danny Ó Súilleabháin. A short version can be heard as 'The Traveller All Over the World' on the CD Irish Voices, sung by the late Frank Harte.

Déaglán Tallon here tells the story of an adventure to Feakle, Co. Clare for a commemoration for Dr. Bill Loughnane, a champion of the Traditional music revival. The air is the common 'Moladh don Athair Máinséil'.

***

The Trip to Feakle

(Air: 'Moladh don Athair Máinséil' or, indeed, 'Beauty Spot Glanlea')

Of life's exhilarations and all things pertaining,
The most invigorating is the prospect of a spree.
So to a kindly invitation to attend a distant station
At Doctor Bill's commemoration we responded with great glee.
Casting off adversity
And whistling optimistically,
We charted comprehensively the route from here to there.
Congregating kegs of porter for sustaining our emotions,
We straightened out for the road and for Fia Choill, County Clare.

Now to make your journey shorter, why not halve it into quarters
And dismount without disorder where hospitality is found?
So we hurried on by halting at houses of debauchery
And entered without faltering, each to his appointed round.
With lubricants intoxicant
Our throats became evocative
And to conductorship provocative practised all our famous airs.
We proceeded thus most pleasantly, to our terminus quite leisurely,
Arriving expeditiously at Fia Choill, County Clare.

There we heard great tunes resounding off the hills and lakes surrounding
And our hearts were full and pounding as we tiptoed towards the bar.
There were fiddlers and fine flautists, like a sympathetic orchestra,
Squeezers of accordions and a harper's grand bazaar.
With polkas, slides and double jigs
We danced with style and elegance
And to our rendering of Gile Mear[60] proclaimed the Irish race.
So our spirits were revitalised and our sore longing satisfied
In a night of great excitement at Fia Choill, County Clare.

Is ar maidín lá ar na mhárach, as daybreak was dawning,
With scratching and much yawning we took the pleasant air.
Being midst scenes of so much beauty we engaged a tipsy courier
To enthral us on a guided tour of the wonders of East Clare.
Round by Maghera and Sliabh an Óir,
From Derrybrien to Loch Gréine's shore
Then lingering at Bal'nahinch we heard mighty piping airs.
At the Black Sticks we met senators who mystified with metaphors
Before anchoring at Kilclaren, near Fia Choill, County Clare.

Going by the bridge at Machaire Bán beneath green leafy awnings,
Past smooth spacious lawns we came to beauteous Glandree.
And there amongst the multitude of female Irish pulchritude
A charming creature we did view with the bearing of a queen.
So proposing with dignity
A marriage of nobility,
Combining the baronies of Tulla and Cúil Aodha,
She considered not hastily, conceding most graciously,
Thus confounding all the merry men of Fia Choill, County Clare.

Níl rí-fhlaith sa tír seo, pé chumasach a chléirigh
A d'árdófadh bórd na féile ós cionn an bainis leagtha romhainn
Príomh-scoth na gcomharsan ag deiliúra go maoiteach
Ag búirthigh len a mbinn guth is ag clagarnach le ceol
Meidhreach aoibhinn meanmnach
Taibhsiúil tréitheach taitneamhach
Le gáir-mhórtais don lánúin is á moladh 'mach ós árd
Is son aicme nach bhuil geanmnach bhí preabaíol agus geamaireacht
Ar an cóisir cuimseach ceanasach i bhFia Choill, Chontae 'n Chláir.

And when life's excitement's ended and I'm filled with deep contentment
I'll hear a summons to attend the Great Celestial Fleadh Cheoil.
And if you'll speed me on my journey with musical accompaniment
Then all my goods redundant are your pleasure to dispose.
Confiscate my property,
Obliterate my memory,
Distribute my skeleton on any handy hill.
Let the dogs chew my marrow, let the wind strew my ashes,
But bury my burning heart in sweet County Clare.

© *Déaglán Tallon*

This settlement in Co. Westmeath would not be everybody's idea of a particularly beautiful place (unless you owned a pub, or were the parish priest). The smell of a tannery would not normally be experienced as perfume (unless you were a bodhrán player); bogland doesn't normally qualify as scenery and geese are hardly a graceful bird in flight. Nor would pigs be described as tender, except after death and some transformation by extreme temperatures. However, inspired by 'Ye nine' (muses—or is this industrial eulogy an early vision of the EEC?) and writing in a mock hedge-schoolmaster style, the Scots W.J. Rankine published such a description of our noble city in his *Songs and Fables* of 1874. Colm O'Lochlainn, compiler of *More Irish Street Ballads,* in 1965 applied the air of 'Preab san Ól, and verse six was added to honour the ancestor of the fleadh cheoil which was held in the city in 1951.

***

The City of Mullingar

(Air: 'Preab san Ól')

Ye may strain your muscles to brag of Brussels,
Of London, Paris or Timbuktu,
Constantinople or Sebastople,
Vienna, New York or Tongaboo,
  Of Copenhagen, Madrid, Kilbeggan,
  Or the capital of the Rooshian Tsar.
  But they're all inferior to the vast superior
  And gorgeous city of Mullingar.

That grand metropolis, so great and populous,
Adorns the regions of sweet Westmeath,
That fertile county which nature's bounty
Has richly gifted with bog and heath.

Them scenes so charming, where snipes a-swarming
Attract the sportsman that comes from far.
And he that wishes may catch fine fishes
In deep Lough Owel close to Mullingar.

I could stray forever by Brosna's river
And watch its waters in their cascades fall,
And ganders swimmin' and lightly skimmin'
O'er the crystal bosom of the royal Canal.
 Or on Thursdays wander 'mid pigs so tender
 And geese and turkeys on many a car,
 Exchangin' pleasantry with the fine bould peasantry
 That throng the market at Mullingar.

Ye nine inspire me, there with rapture fire me
To sing the buildings both old and new,
The majestic courthouse, the spacious workhouse,
The church and steeple which adorn the view.
 There's a barracks airy for the military
 Where the brave repose from the toils of war;
 Five schools, a nunnery and a thrivin' tannery
 In the gorgeous city of Mullingar.

The railway station with admiration
I next must mention in terms of praise,
With ingin' growlin' and white steam howlin',
Strike each beholder with wild amaze.
 And then there's Main Street that neat and clean street,
 With its rows of gas lamps that shine afar;
 I could spake a lecture in the architecture
 Of the gorgeous city of Mullingar.

The men of genius contemporaneous,
Approach spontaneous this favoured spot
Where good society and great variety
Of entertainment is to be got.
 The local quality for hospitality
 And conviviality unequalled are;
 And from December until November
 There's much diversion there in Mullingar.

So my effusion will now enthuse on
The culture there 'mongst these dacent souls
Whose-harmonic ex-e-ge-sis lured in the exodus
From Dublin that became the first Fleadh cheoil;
    With fiddles screeching and pipes a-bleating,
    Flutes, box and bodhráns in every bar,
    Fleadh Cowboys bawling, and mammies calling
    Their teenage daughters home from Mullingar.

And now in conclusion, I make allusion
To such beauteous females as do here abound;
Celestial creatures with gorgeous features
And taper ankles that do skim the ground.
    But my pen offends me, the theme transcends me—
    My muses' powers are too weak by far:
    It would take Catullus or perhaps Tibullus
    To be proper praising o-of Mullingar.

Verse 6 © Fintan Vallely

And so we leap close to the present day where we know everything. Mullingar is no longer the finest city in the world, The Reeks are no longer the most spectacular mountains. Or so other people's tourist propaganda tells us. But we are sick to death of being leprechauns to be leered at, and the Bórd Fáilte PR brochures are not the healthiest source of information about one's-self. Bríain O'Rourke wrote this fine denunciation of the Tourist-game claptrap. Reeking of Mullingarism, and reminiscent of comedian Frank Kelly's anthropologically-focused, fictional 'Ballygroppel', 'Ballykilferret' and 'Kilsnobbery', it is a fine reminder of our chauvinism as we groped towards the 21st century.

***

Drumsnot, Beauty Spot
(Air: somewhat like 'The Wild Colonial Boy' only different)

Oh come all ye pleasant fellow peasants
    And listen to my song;
It has but twenty verses,
    Even if it seems three times as long.
Oh, lend me your ears while I shed my tears
    About the place where I was got;
For it's likely that you haven't much of a clue
    About the place they call Drumsnot.

Where my birthplace lies beneath Irish skies
    Isn't easy to explain.
It's not in The Pale or the Golden Vale,
    Nor yet in the Central Plain.
It affords no view of mountainy hues
    And for sure it's no beauty spot,
And to date no county has claimed the bounty
    For confessing to contain Drumsnot.

Oh, on Inniscarra, on Gougane Barra,
    On Macroom and on Omagh town,
God poured out air of a fragrance fair
    That gained them high renown.

On King Williamstown he showered sweetness down,
    On Lough Neagh and Glenlea the lot,
But those rare perfumes were all well consumed
    By the time that he reached Drumsnot.

Ah, but that lavish matron—savage nature—
    Drumsnot did not neglect,
For its pebbled fields with wild, splendid weeds
    Are gaudily bedecked:
Them thistles, thorns and *búachaláns*
    Would be an ugly blot
Upon the face of any place
    Excepting fair Drumsnot.

And all around wildlife abounds
    And leaps and creeps and crawls,
And prowls and scowls and growls and howls
    And fights and bites and bawls.
It shrieks and reeks, it yells and smells,
    And kills and the devil knows what.
O when nature calls, it's a free for all
    In the jungle around Drumsnot.

Now to sing of the birds, I have no words
    To express quite how I feel,
For the sweetest notes in their cheeky throats
    Are the fivers that they steal:
The sly magpie it is that rules the sky
    And ruins every garden and plot,
And every feathered songster is a fully-fledged gangster
    On the rampage round Drumsnot.

Oh, we hold no Fleadh, we've no cinema
    To enliven desolate moods.
And Tim Lyons couldn't grouse about our 'atin' house
    That never heard tell of Fast Food.
We've a TV set that hasn't got RTÉ yet
    And a gaming machine with no slot;
Like a building site in the middle of the night,
    The main street of Drumsnot.

Oh, now you might guess that Drumsnot's a place
    Where old customs are held dear,
And you'd be dead right for our faction fights
    Cut our numbers by half each year.
As for the Gaelic tongue, you'd as soon hear sung
    The speech of the Hotten-tot.
In fact we're distinguished for unspeakable English
    In these backwaters of Drumsnot.

If you play the fiddle, or dance or diddle
    Or meddle on box or bones,
Let it be quite clear, you're not wanted here,
    You'd be pelted with sticks, bricks and stones.
There's a céilí band in some part of this land
    Whose visit will ne'er be forgot:
They lost their piano and their leading tenor
    In the Carnival at Drumsnot.

Oh, in Ireland's fight for her birthright
    We have had no glorious share,
For the Black and Tans with their tanks and vans
    Never even knew we were there.
Now they've gone away, and 'tis sad to say
    Nothing has changed one jot:
For except for the Greens no TD has been
    To canvass in Drumsnot.

Our hedge-master died in eighteen-o-five
    And since then we have had no school,
And for all we see of CIÉ
    We might as well be in Kabul.
Ah, but soon we might get th'oul 'lectric light—
    And then again we might not—
The Christmas mail arrives without fail
    About Easter in Drumsnot.

Oh, a telephone ki-osk or a Shi-ite mosque
    Would be equal novelty here,
So our smoking signals and homing pigeons
    Our urgent messages bear.
And no motor car has yet got that far
    For the Spring Show could justly allot,
For sheer scope and size, a major prize
    To each pothole around Drumsnot.

We've no B&Bs, no facilities
    For the stranger touring round,
No *céad míle fáilte* about here will halt you
    If you tread on our tainted ground.
If you're tracing ancestors in parish registers
    Here you won't find a lot:
For marriage, be japers, is the rarest caper
    In the Parish of Drumsnot.

If you've a low opinion of our dominion
    Please don't broadcast your point of view,
For although the locals seem like yobs and yokels
    They have their sense of pride too.
A bass baritone of twenty stone
    Dropped a hint our singing wasn't too hot:
Well he was singin' falsetto when he left our ghetto—
    And he's never forgot Drumsnot.

Oh, 'twas in Drumsnot that I was begot
    And spent my curious childhood days,
But now those youthful deeds from my mind recede
    In an alcoholical haze.
For when I grew a man, I worked out a flawless plan—
    I teamed up with a well-endowed mot
Whose father owned 'The Rag and Bone',
    The only lounge bar in Drumsnot.

Oh by the sewage pump near the rubbish dump
    We courted each other well,
And we got engaged after seven days,
    For she couldn't stand the smell.

There came a day, of course, in the month of May
    When we tied the fatal knot:
The wedding do was crubeens for two,
    Top cuisine in Drumsnot.

Now we live in a cabin with the thatch in ribbons
    and the rent we can barely pay,
And all the roses around the door
    won't keep the wolf away.
And all my dreams of pints so creamy
    alas they have come to naught,
For supplies of stout they did soon run out
    in the only pub in Drumsnot

Oh I wish I was far from the Shamrock Shore
    In some place where I might find work,
But I tried too late to emigrate,
    For I missed the last lift to Cork.
So to settle down in my native town
    Has become my doleful lot,
To sink my roots in my hobnail boots
    In this boghole called Drumsnot.

Now as you all know some years ago
    Big blundering Uncle Sam
Tried to lift fifty-one of his native sons
    Held hostage beyond in Iran.
Ah, but isn't it sad when 'twas all the fad
    That the whole bloody world forgot
To send rescue choppers for us poor fuckers
    Marooned inside Drumsnot.

And so at last I must conclude, arrest
    And terminate this desperate ditty.
And I hope that you, good people true,
    By now feel for me some pity.
And when at last my life is past
    And my bones have to moulder and rot,
I pray God on high they won't have to lie
    In the cemetery of Drumsnot.

No tourist trade would be complete without allegations of destruction and pollution. A decade or so ago someone came up with the brilliant idea of opening a gold mine in Co. Mayo. Wonderful! But there was terrible opposition. The begrudgers said they didn't want one, the hoteliers already had a goldmine—tourists with American Express cards. After a long legal struggle, and years of filling the rivers with cyanide poisoning to discourage shirty fisherfolk, nosey gawkers and other work-shy foreign tramps, the low-class wealth was abandoned and the panhandlers moved on. No doubt when people get sick and tired of travelling to look at each others' 'mountains and skies' and shapes of water, some future entrepreneur will have another go.

***

Your Place Or Mine?

(Air: 'The Bogs of Shanaheever')

Oh come all ye Irish citizens and listen to my story
Of developments and happenings now causing great furore.
They say Connacht's hills and valleys and St. Patrick's holy mountain
Are stuffed full of golden guineas nearly ready for the countin'.

Now the strange thing is that here and there, there are a few objectors
Who distrust the mining companies and frown on the prospectors—they
Don't seem to see our problems could all find a quick solution
At the negligible cost of long-term chemical pollution.

Oh the chosen few among us will be rich as old King Midas,
And the modest price we'll all pay is—some cyanide inside us.
The improvement in our diet will make everyone a glutton
With the subtle taste of arsenic of Connamara mutton.

Those big company directors will give ministers a handshake
And they'll set the wheels in motion to transform the barren landscape,
And the local men will be employed on JCB and dumper
But they'll carry off the profits to Hong Kong and Kuala Lumpur.
Oh they'll rip the landscape inside out and give it all a new look

194

And them tourist types will come no more to Louisburgh or Doolough,
And there's no way you can stop it 'cos they wanna and they gonna
And by God they'll leave their trademark on the hills round Cornamona.

And the eerie peace and quiet will at last, thank god, be shattered
When the dynamite's exploded and the rocks are crushed and battered,
And the toxic waste washed off the land will cause efficient slaughter
Of the rainbow trout and salmon that infest our inland waters.

We'll be modernised and civilised, by God it makes me chuckle.
We'll repudiate our past, and we'll forget the *cúpla focail.*
When the new golden God makes each one a true believer,
Then we'll soon see the last of the bogs of Shanaheever.

*The original song can be heard on Brian O'Rourke's When I Grow Up,
and the air on Sean Garvey's CD Out of the Ground.*

Part 16: Come All Ye Bould Saily-ors

THE SEALINK SONG

In the aftermath of *The Herald of Free Enterprise* ferry sinking in Zebrugge in 1987, the ferry companies to both parts of Ireland began operating an aircraft-style safety procedure which is still rigorously gone through as the boats cast off. The object is to show passengers how to put on a life-jacket, get into the lifeboat, etc. However, the language used for these PA broadcasts seems a bit over the top. Since it takes you the whole journey to find your way back to your seat after a normal visit to the toilet, and since you get lost every time you get out of your seat unless you bring a ball of thread, how could you possibly memorise the way to a 'Muster Station'?

***

The Sealink Song

(Air: 'Let Mister Maguire Sit Down')

Come all you jolly mariners, and welcome all aboard
This new vessel on which we've spent all we can afford.
For your safety and security, we've jackets, belts and boats
In case of the possibility we cease to stay afloat.
We have twice as many life supports as you could ever use,
Finely tailored jackets personally fitted by our crew
Who'll delight in acting escort if occasion says we do
Have to drop you forty feet in rafts into the briny blue.

Of course we've ample capability to seat yous all on board
On barstools, bunks and benches, stairs and lying round the floor.
We've video cartoons and ads., and Duty Free galore
And we practise MAYDAY[61] warnings to prevent you getting bored.
For your comfort and convenience we've got restaurants and bars
To ease your separations from your juggernauts and cars.
Our prices are competitive—we sell the cheapest jar[62]
If you're prepared to queue for miles like refugees of war.

CHORUS:
Oh the roaring of the engines, Oh the black smoke in the air,
Oh the reek of burning clutches as the hasty drivers swear.
Oh the joys of shuffling heel to toe, and sleep upright in chairs,
Oh! Sure who would fly when ferries try so hard to show they care?

And if mother nature strikes and you have call to use the loo
Whether simply for the toilet—or an after-drinking spew—
We fit you out with clothing-pegs, gas masks and rubber boots
For as you know at sea we're sometimes plagued by blocked-up sewers.[63]
And if by some unlikely chance we hit a storm or gale
We've brandy, port and sickly bags if you turn green or pale.
We've expert para-medics and, for leaning-over rails,[64]
Buckets, mops and canvas sacks—if all of these should fail.

But sinking fast this decade is the image of the boat,
As undermined by tunnels now we barely stay afloat,
As people up in airplanes[65] in great armchairs interlope
Between the nations to get sunshine just like presidents and popes.
No more keening on the dockside, no more three-day American wakes[66]
With their rum and poteen riddled, wretched, rabid, roarin' rakes.
We may leave the sea for postcards and for poet laureates,
For without a wheeze of salty breeze these days we emigrate.
CHORUS

One morning in 1985 (a good year for songs) the yacht of Charles J. Haughey, sometime High King of Ireland, crash-landed on the Mizzen Head off Co. Cork as he was rushing home to his mansion for the Sunday fry. All sorts of theories abound as to why this happened. One allegation concerned a submarine game by NATO in the Irish Sea playpool that weekend: recognising another pleasure boat, and there being no trawlers left to pull underwater, it is supposed that they might have fouled up its radar.[67] Hero of the adventure was the Mizzen's lighthouse keeper[68] who gave up a night's sleep to counsel the survivors by torch light, but all this was overshadowed as the craven Party Faithful flocked down to Baltimore to witness their Boss being winched ashore and dried out on the pier—all timed perfectly to get the national Radio's Sunday *One O'Clock News*.

***

Charles The Navigator

(Air: 'Slattery's Mounted Foot')

Columbus found America, Harry Krishna found Nepal,
Australia was found by Captain Cooke, and the Vikings found us all,
But the greatest thing in geography the world has ever read
Is how Charles the Navigator—just discovered Mizzen Head.
A man of deepest dedication to his conquered land
Charles tried taypots[69], talks and lunch but failed to take command.
He studied up his history and Saint Brendan struck him most.
"The answer is," says he, "To find new land off Ireland's coast"—SO,

CHORUS:
Down from Dublin came the settlers' cars and vans
To Baltimore to file for plots of fresh-discovered land.
They wore *I Love Charlie* badges,
They owned pubs and farms and shops.
For Charles the Navigator, they had given up the lot.

In Dingle all September those tars sat poised in vain.
They prayed to Brendan day and night for him to stop the rain.
Till finally on the twenty-eighth a fresh wind cleared the sky
And Charles on the MV[70] *Hennessy* to Ireland waved good-bye.
Engines powered by heated air made sure they couldn't fail,
While great long-winded speeches gave propulsion to their sail.
The latest MRBI[71] gear was mounted all around
To guarantee their odyssey with glory would be crowned, AND
CHORUS

At nine o'clock a blackness fell, astronomy filled the night,
Intense galactic observations made their guts so tight
That rations had to be passed around till clock and calendar changed
To find them on the twenty-ninth, dishevelled and deranged.
NATO was playin 'space invaders' on their radar screens,
Young Conor played the figurehead of this rakish barque so green,
When all at once 'a sickening crunch'[72] helped them realise
They'd struck uncharted shores at last, the tears came to their eyes, AND
CHORUS

A native of that rugged rock was witness to this scene.
He telegraphed the *National Geographic* magazine,
While our explorers floundered round in water to the hip
To rescue posters, flags and chequebooks from their sunken ship.
The Mizzen's brave night-watchman kept their spirits up with poems
That he read out by flashlamp until RTÉ could come
To witness for all Ireland, just as we get out of bed—
Charles the Navigator landin' on the Mizzen Head, AND
CHORUS

© Fintan Vallely

Part 17: The Sports Pages

Miltown Malbay in County Clare is the hometown of the (late) renowned piper and satirical songster Willie Clancy. It has a football team whose fortunes, like those of any in rural Ireland, rise and fall with the emigration graph. This factor wipes out all the painstaking cultural work that goes on in any community in fact—everyone of the age of seventeen or eighteen seems to disappear in the one weekend each year, for more or less good. There is nothing left behind and the will of local teachers is sapped by the apparent uselessness of the task. Speaking at the St. Patrick's Day parade in Miltown in 1987, Brendan Daly, a local Fianna Fáil TD, pledged to "…stamp out the scourge of emigration that is decimating rural Ireland". At approximately the same time, addressing the St. Patrick's Day parade in new York, his boss, Charles J. Haughey was pledging to "…make urgent representations to get as many US immigrant visas for the Irish as possible". There is of course, no contradiction between these two sentiments, it only seems that way, and the English language has a word for it—antinomy. In that year, however, Brendan Daly was winning, and so Miltown had a formidable GAA team which won the Clare senior county championship after a breathtaking match against St. Bricín's of Lisdoonvarna. Miltown's supporters were as numerous and frenzied as you would get at an Ireland World Cup game, and the high charge they induced in the Ennis stadium guaranteed victory.

The trainer was the local bank's then assistant manager, Gerry Fitzgerald; Liz Curtin is a local glass ball medium; and the then bank manager himself lit the victory pyre in Miltown's square that night—an impressive inferno of old furniture and car tyres located strategically between two sets of petrol pumps. Saffron and Wine are the team's colours. Miltown defeated Cooraclare in the same championship in 1959 (but it didn't take place till 1960—a long, long story), the Miltown team wore the traditional jerseys but St. Bricín's wore a very sexy, close-fitting soccer-style gear which did them no good among the hard men of Miltown. Lisdoonvarna is famed for its 'matchmaking' festival (nothing to do with Maguire and Patterson), a kind of annual elephants' graveyard which introduces canny, single, ancient men and women for a week of drinking in the forlorn hope that they might go out with a bang.

***

Saffron and Wine

(Air: 'Erin Go Bráth')

You'll hear of Benfica wherever you go,
Of the bould Balesteros and John McEnroe,
But I'd walk past them all and I'd pick any time
Those wild Miltown heroes in Saffron and Wine.

A team of distinction and skill in their play
They'd raised through the rafters all standards the day
That they last were the victors back in fifty-nine
When they tied Cooraclare up in Saffron and Wine.

On laurels for twenty-five years they'd laid back
Till the patrons demanded they have a fresh crack,
For the whole population had started to pine
For a sup from a cup full of Saffron and wine.

They consulted their mystic—Liz Curtin—to see
What she thought their 'eighty-five chances would be.
She looked in her ball and says, "Here's what I find—
Our local bank branch coloured Saffron and Wine."
So, behind bullet-proof glass, secret new ways to train
That incorporated the lost hay and rain
Were hatched on nest of fresh banknotes and coin
And computed a victory for Saffron and Wine.

From drink, sex and drugs all those young men abstained,
From lard and potatoes and travel to Spain,

Till on the big day out in Ennis they lined,
Fifteen wild heroes in Saffron and Wine.

They burst on to the pitch to a tumultuous cheer.
The Lisdoon supporters all gasped at their gear—
New jerseys and togs with a Paris design
And flags, banners and pandas in Saffron and Wine.

For all the long hour Miltown were everywhere.
They hardly let Bricín's touch that bag of air.
Like gazelles usin' radar they'd won at half time
And brought home the cup full of Saffron and Wine.

Miltown that night was just like the Bogside,
Black smoke and bonfires reflected the pride
Of the town the matchmakers could not match in kind
With those wild Miltown heroes in Saffron and Wine.

© *Fintan Vallely*

The term 'Pool' in these islands, because of the climate, does not refer to what it refers to in Australia or California. It is a game played by men with balls and sticks inside a frame with legs covered in green cloth. These devices, found in the scruffiest rooms in public houses everywhere, are used to while away the hours of unemployed boredom and represent the best way to combine the spending of a wet day, all your money, the stretching of a pint to Germanic proportions, and exchanging all the latest rumours and lies. The practice became addictive in the 70s and 80s, achieving highs of popularity during the televising of big tournaments, in much the same way that soccer becomes popular during World Cups. Pool is alleged to have wrecked people, music, homes and conversation, and, capitalising here on the prejudice, Con Ó Drisceoil, introduces all the ills laid at its door.

***

The Pool Song

(Air: Traditional, based on 'The Clonmel Cows', from Cúil Aodha, Co. Cork)

May the Lord upon high who rules the sky
Look down on our pubs and bars,
For the people therein, both women and men,
They're neglecting their pints and their jars.
The crack there is bad, the atmosphere sad,
Every wan has a face like a mule;
And all they can do is grab an ould cue
And start playin' a game of Pool.

Well, when I was a boy, 'twas always my joy
To visit the pub each night.
There were arguments, scraps and killings perhaps
And everyone thought they was right.
There were badgers and dogs and men from the bogs
And young fellas actin' the tool;
But now there's no crack, for every man-jack
Has their arse in the air playing Pool.

To the rural ale-house, after milkin' the cows,
The customers made their way;
And there would dwell and drink till they fell
While the fiddles and pipes they did play.
The jigs and the reels and the rattling of heels
And the polkas and slides were the rule;
But now there's no chance of a tune or a dance,
Cos everyone's playin' th'ould pool.

Now this Pool you will find is a game designed
For foolish illiterate louts.
You puts in your four bob and press an ould knob
And a big shower of balls rattles out.
They're placed on the table, and then, if you're able,
You knock them all into a hole.
More money goes in, you start over again,
Till you lose every bob of your dole.

In the Irish Free State all the people are bate
From watching and playing this game.
In their necks they have cricks that no doctor can fix
And their backs and their shoulders are maimed.
Their arses protrude in a manner most lewd
From being hoisted aloft in the air,
And their eyeballs are sore, and dripping in gore,
And they act in a manner most queer.

So if you meet a young man whose face it is wan
And his eyes have a vacant stare;
If his jaw-bone is slack and his head is thrown back,
And he can't tell a cob from a mare;
With his nostrils dilated, his brow corrugated,
His manners like those of a fool;
Then your shirt you can bet that you have just met
A man that's gone mad from the pool.

This song can be heard on Con Ó Drisceoil's Spoons Murder…CD, and on Jimmy Crowley's album The Boys Of Fairhill (Mulligan, 1977).

Part 18: The Land Of Irish Presidents

THE RONALD REAGAN BAR

In 1984 the President of the USA announced a second coming to Ireland[73] —for purely nostalgic purposes, of course. Coincidentally it was an election year and the Irish-American vote may have been of passing interest to him, so to authenticate the process he had to be proven to be (southern) Irish. The CIA found him a baptismal entry in a Catholic chapel in Ballyporeen, and lo and behold—his ancestors, didn't they come from there. Much newspaper hoo-ha surrounded the visit, and as part of the propaganda run-up, pictures were released of the entry in the church's register to prove his title. To the begrudging whingers in our midst the name certainly looked like 'Ryan', but it had been altered to look like 'Reagan'. And the other question on sceptical lips was: "How come Ronnie Reagan, a non-Catholic, claims ancestry in a Catholic Reagan in 1847?" The soup kitchens had thrived that year, run by people from the wealthier classes and by religious bodies. Wild rumours abounded that many's the St. Paul conversion took place over a lip-smacking bowl of steaming broth. Hunger is a great sauce, they say, and the odd thread of a second-hand breeches or smock for the heat no doubt was a very sensible swop if you were fit to eat the harness off a nightmare and feeling like a brass monkey in Siberia. Swopping the alleged hereafter for the certain present seems not a bad deal, considering it was never religion that was being fought about in the first place. But God was still very, very political in those far-off days. And then Ronnie's PR team came up as well with a most wonderful icing on his pedigree cake— they discovered that he was in fact descended from King Brian Boru, 11th

206

century High King of Ireland, now buried in Armagh where they call the Dole after him. They omitted the information that this was a very long time ago, long enough for everybody in Ireland to have some of his genes, but that's showbiz. In Galway, while Ron was being conferred with an honorary doctorate in something or other, intelligent university staff on the next block conferred a similar degree on an ass. In Dublin about 40,000 people turned out to a protest carnival against his visit and hardly anybody turned out to cheer him (a long way from Saint John F. Kennedy's triumphal entry to Dublin in 1963). Ron didn't even drink the pint he was photographed with in 'The Ronald Reagan Bar'—it was tasted by a CIA man and then thrown down the sink. It was Smithwicks too. At the end of it all the event brought prosperity to the town and they got a couple of new phone boxes out of the deal. The air is that of 'The Boys from the County Armagh'.

***

The Ronald Reagan Bar

(Air: 'The Boys from the County Armagh')

There's one fair county in Ireland
With memories so glorious and grand
Where tourists lavished their bounty
And bought mud packs[74] from Erin's green land.
I love Ballyporeen's wee chapel,
Its chip-shop and petrol pumps too;
Did youse know my ancestors came from there?
Descended from Brian Boru?

CHORUS:
It's my old Irish home
Far across the foam
Although I'd never been there;
To love it I had grown.
No matter where we plundered
In cities near and far,
Sure me heart is at home in ould Ireland
In the Ronald Reagan Bar.[75]

I'd heard of that part of my Kingdom
'Round Newtown, Forkhill, Crossmaglen,[76]
El Salvador wouldn't be in it,
A nightmare to peace-lovin' men.
So I talked of the County Tipperary,
Of shamrock potatoes and ham,
Of the millions of half-Irish voters
All watchin' me visit Ireland.
CHORUS

We've stuck to the family traditions
Picked up in that soup kitchen grand,
And here's my advice for your freedom:
The Greens and the Reds youse should ban.
We own half the world since we left yis
But Patrick we've never forgot:
Won't yis share the ould sod with yer grandson
And give NATO and Cruise a wee plot?
CHORUS

© *Fintan Vallely*

John Maguire of Cork took the national cynicism about Ronnie much further, introducing all the Imperialistic interventions of the US in his imprecation here. This was after all the decade in which a great tableau of malicious manipulation of mindless minorities in the interests of maintenance of US power had gone on in central America—and everybody in Ireland knew about it.

Hey Ronnie Reagan

I remember the show twenty-one years ago
When John Kennedy paid us a visit,
Now the world's re-arranged—not improved, only changed—
But our heart's in the same place—or is it?

CHORUS:
Hey Ronnie Reagan, I'm black and I'm pagan,
I'm gay and I'm left and I'm free.
I'm a non-fundamentalist, environmentalist,
Please don't bother me.

You're so cool playin' poker with death as the joker,
You've nerve but you don't reassure us,
With those paranoid vistas of mad Sandinistas,
Are you really defendin' Honduras?
You'll be wearin' the green down at Ballyporeen,
The town of the little potato.
Put your arms around Garret and dangle your carrot,
But you'll never get me to join NATO.
CHORUS

Do you share my impression, the world's in recession
With rather too much unemployment?
Still with Pershing and Cruise we'll have nothing to lose
But millions in missile deployment.

We can dig shelter holes when we've bartered our souls
For security then we can shovel
While the myth of our dreams turns to nightmares it seems
From the White House straight back to the hovel.
CHORUS

Since the Irish dimension has won your attention
I ask myself just what's your game.
Do your eyes share the tears of our last fifteen years
Or is that just a vote-catcher's gleam?
Your dollars may beckon, but I think we should reckon
The cost of accepting your gold:
If we join your alliance, what price our defiance
What's left if freedom is sold?
CHORUS

This song can be heard on Christy Moore's giveaway 45 rpm disc associated with his Ride On album. The song has also appeared in Frank Connolly's The Christy Moore Songbook, and Christy Moore's own One Voice - My Life in Song.

Iraq, 1991, was not George Bush senior's first attempt at military immortality. He had earlier found a soft touch in invading Panama. A gullible public seem to have been confused enough to almost say nothing as Georgie sold them the notion that the suppliers of drugs (well, some small number of them) were in fact responsible for the American drug problem. Poverty and homelessness weren't considered. It really seemed like blaming the suppliers of drink on alcoholism, or coffee-producers on heart disease... Where do you stop—invade Turkey (or some other tobacco producer) to stamp out lung-cancer? Panama's petty boss General Noriega, with whom George Bush, as head of the CIA, had once worked closely at a time when that body was itself interested in promoting the drug trade, was arrested. Afterwards Jesse Jackson reported to Congress that 1,200 civilians were killed by US forces in the invasion—200 more than were killed by Chinese authorities in Tiennamen Square in Peking the previous year.

The end of the debacle came when Noriega got sanctuary in the good old democratic Vatican Embassy, only leaving after the G.I's. played loud recordings of Peter Brooke practising 'Clementine'. The event got George back into the history books after a disastrous period when, with the kaleidoscopic changes in the Soviet Union, Michael Gorbachov was hardly ever off the airwaves, and George was never on. He got his biggest bite at the cherry in Iraq, and, even by the time Americans had decided that his five-year audition had been quite enough and voted him out, he got a last nibble at the pip by sending troops to Somalia. This song speculates what might have happened had George decided to stamp out drinking, and its attendant destructive effects on the health of the American nation.

***

Panamania

(Air: 'Trippin' up to Claudy', etc.)

As autumn turned to winter, nineteen eighty-nine,
Eastern Europe put aside barbed wire and seemed inclined
To haggle out a path where people wouldn't be entwined
By borders, ideologies or any kind of line.

But for every kilometre this new thinking strode ahead.
Georgie Bush replied with an "I TOLD YOU SO" tirade.
But the TV news ignored him and he sank into despair
While his desperate doctors wondered how to get him on the air.

CHORUS:
Pan-a man-i-a's the new disease today,
Democracy, hypocrisy's a canny game to play.
While Moscow opened curtains in attempts to light the dark,
Georgie Porgie's acted out Napoleon Bonaparte.

So in desperation George consulted Ronnie's Mirror on the Wall
Which had predicted bombs in Libya, and a summit with Pope Paul.
He asked it, "How do I show them who's the fairest of them all?"
It said: "DON'T touch smokes or coffee—You'll be safe with alcohol."

SO, he considered Pernod, poteen, vodka, saki and the Greek
And Turkish schnapps that rots your liver and destroys the workin' week.
He thought: "Prohibition's failed before—so we'll stamp it out at source,
And we'll start with Scotch for that will bring the media out in force."
CHORUS

SO, the fleet was sent to Scotland on this propaganda lark
They parked their tanks on Glasgow Green and put their tents on West End Park,
But the *Teachers* rang the *Bells*, and the *Black and White* dogs barked,
And *Johnnie Walker* escaped on a *White Horse* to *Highland Park*.

The Rangers saw that he was on the rocks and rallied round
In diplomatic spirit to protect him from his hounds.
But when Uncle Sam bombarded them with a million watts of sound
The strains of 'Father Murphy' brought their courage tumbling down.
CHORUS

Now bound in chains, Johnnie rots in Miami jail,
A monument to Reagan by *Black Bush* and *Famous Quayle*.
But invasion's not persuasion, so still Georgie yearned for fame,
For Europe's sweeping changes were for real and not a game.

© *Fintan Vallely*

212

Part 19: National Affairs

HO CHARLIUM

Leaving aside mere trivia like Nelson Mandela's release and the reunification of Germany, undoubtedly the most astounding happening of the 1980s was the election of Mary Robinson to the Presidency in Ireland, Backed by the Labour Party and aided by a Liberal/Left coalition she went from odds-against, to favourite, back to neck in neck, and on, amid 'exciting scenes', to win. Her victory was remarkable in that she had devoted much of her working life as a barrister to principle stands on Family Law cases, the constitutionality/legality of contraception and divorce, and on the right to choice and information on the issue of abortion—all inflammatory subjects throughout the '70s and '80s, particularly in the aftermath of the apparition of JPII in '79. She represented the efforts of intelligent people to shake a parasitic church structure off the back of Irish political life and, amazingly, won the day. Her own integrity should have been enough to do that, but it took the hand of the Lord—in the guise of her opponent, the favourite Brian Lenihan—to give her the necessary edge. Brian's loyal supporters emptied the pisspots out the top windows in an effort to stem her popularity but in the end it was he himself, his body surgically reconstructed at enormous expense for the fray, who blunderingly directed his own downfall. Mary Robinson's standing threw the "not until Ireland is free" lobby into scenes of confusion and self doubt—her middle class image for them transcended the memory of her

213

having been on every campaign for women's rights that they had been on, and forgotten was the fact that she was the barrister currently taking the censorious 'Section 31' of the Broadcasting Act to the European Court.

From very early in the campaign however, other long knives were out to get Brian. First he was accused of making an out-of-order phone call to the then current President. This he foolishly denied, despite the fact that it had been reported at the time, and he had put it 'on the record' with a politics student called Duffy to whom he had given an interview. Next thing it was all published in *The Irish Times* edited by Conor Brady and, like Eric Cantana, the shit hit the fan. Forced to resign his Ministership of Defence, he didn't, and had to be sacked, but his party still supported him as their chosen Presidential candidate after he reneged on his double thinking in what he described as "mature recollection". A quite separate, but sleazy, smear campaign was run in support of him by SPUC supporters who called Mary R an 'abortionist'. A Fianna Fáil Minister wondered aloud would she be contemplating running an abortion clinic in the Presidential palace while yet another wondered on a radio programme why she wasn't home minding the children like a proper Irishwoman instead of gallivanting the streets making a career for herself. The latter gentleman—Pádraig Flynn—proved Brian's downfall. She couldn't have organised it better herself, indeed, at the Robinson victory rally Pádraig got a special vote of thanks. 'Charlium' is a reference to the Taoiseach of the day, Charles Haughey, and the style of the song is from the original of the species—a 'macaronic' 1920s campus song from the U.S.A. called 'Ho Rogerum', wherein it was the custom to turn line-end words into mock Latin.

***

Ho Charlium

(Air: 'Ho Rogerum')

WELL, I'm here to tell the story
Of the race to Phoenix Park-i-um,
The Presidential lark-i-um, Ho Char-li-um.
It began when Paddy Hillery
Was called in from the dark-i-um
And tould to disembark-i-um, Ho Charli-ol-i-um,
Tould to disembark-i-um, Ho Charlium.

214

THREE stables entered horses
And the country ran a tote-i-um,
Betting was in vote-i-um, Ho Charlium.
The commentators knew the form,
Well prepared with quote-i-um,
And poisoned anec-dote-i-um, Ho Charlium.

CHORUS:
Ho Charli-um, Ho Charli-o-li-um,
Divorce and contra-cep-ti-um.

FIRST the Bruton stud was full of tension,
Rows and apoplexium ,
Not ready for elects-i-um, Ho Charlium.
Oul Garret didn't want the job
For he had intell-ects-i-um
And his retrospect-i-um, Ho Charli-ol-i-um,
And his retrospectium, Ho Charli-um.

AND SO when they sat down togeth-er
To look at their portfolium
What a gaping hole-i-um, Ho Charlium.
The safest for the role-i-um was Austin Currie-ol-i-um,
A squatter from Tyrol-i-um, Ho Charlium.

CHORUS
Ho Charli-um, Ho Charli-o-li-um,
Divorce and contra-cep-ti-um.

BUT there were those in this soci'ty
Who'd been belted with a crozium,
And tangled up in a rosary-um, Ho Charlium.
Women who'd been snubbed for years
Who hadn't had it so cosy-um
And Ban-di-era Ros-si-um, Ho Charl-i-ol-i-um,
Bandiera Ross-a, Ho Charlium.

SAYS they "If Fianna Fáil gets in,
We'll choke with claustro-phobi-um,
We're sick of De-Val-ob-i-um, Ho Charlium.

And we're tired of Opus Dope-i-um
And Knights of Colum-ope-i-um,
We'll put our faith and hope-ium
In Robinsop-i-um."

CHORUS:
Ho Charlium, Ho Charli-ol-e-um,
Divorce and contra-cep-ti-um.

THEN the Kinsealy Stud selector thought
"Our chances are red hott-i-um,
To beat this scarlet mott-i-um," Ho Charlium.
"This job is for our man, an Irish-speaking patrioticum.
For women it is not-i-um," Ho Charl-i-ol-i-um,
"For women it is not-i-um," Ho Charlium."

And So they picked their finest orator
And sent him for a service-um
To Mayo in Americum[77], Ho Charlium.
He got new plugs and filters
And filters for his ol-I-um.
He said he'd top the poll-I-um,
Ho Charlium.

CHORUS
Ho Charlium, Ho Charli-ol-e-um,
Divorce and contra-cep-ti-um.

AND SO three horses fly out from the tapes,
And leading is the Westmeath one,
Glory be to backing, HO Charlium.
RED, Robbin's thirty lengths behind—
The Squatter's eatin' daisy-um,
But he was backed both ways-i-um, Ho Charli-ol-i-um,
He was backed both waysium Ho Charl-i-um.

BUT leader's horsey faltered at the jumps,
And then it threw the head-i-um,
Right outside the stad-i-um, Ho Charl-i-um.
IT tipped him off in Beech-ers,[78]

In muck he was a wade-i-um,
Thanks to Conor Brady-um, Ho Charlium.

CHORUS
Ho Charlium, Ho Charli-ol-e-um,
Divorce and contra-cep-ti-um

AND Robbin galloped past him
In the cloud of allegat-i-um
And left him to his fate-i-um, Ho Charl-i-um.
While Duffy circus vul-tures ripped him up and slated him
It looked like he was bate-i-um, Ho Charli-ol-i-um,
Looked like he was bate-i-um, Ho Charli-i-um.

NEXT THING the stewards bowed to pressure
From the ruthless Des O'Mall-ey-um,
A boner from Hal-Al-i-um[79], Ho Charlium.
They took his saddle and his whip but said
They'd back him in the Dáil-i-um,
Double-think and all -i-um, Ho Charlium.

CHORUS
Ho Charlium, Ho Charli-ol-e-um,
Divorce and contra-cep-ti-um.

BUT he fought them off and mounted up
In scenes of in-surr-ect-i-um,
He promised he'd reveal it all if we elected, hum
CON-cussion had shook up his brain,
And left him quite perplex-i-um.
It caused mature recc-lects-i-um, Ho Char-li-ol-i-um,
Caused mature recc-lects-i-um Ho Charlium.

SO-O once more there's nothing in it—
Westmeath Leader and Red Robbin—All
All forgotten in a minute, Ho Charl-i-um.
"The lord is on our side," he cried[80]
To Party faithful sobbin'-um,
At every church they're mobbin' him, Ho Charli-ol-i-um,
At every church they're mobbin him, Ho Charlium.

But SUDDENLY—a flock of
    emotionally deprived
    unwashed
    unfed
    unloved
    unwanted
    undernourished
Rickety babies crying "MAMMY!"
Were released by Pádraig Flynn-i-um,
Stooping low to win-i-um, Ho Charlium
BUT they made such a din that
It was a mortal sin-i-um,
Put Leader's chances in the bin, Ho Charli-ol-i-um.

CHORUS
Ho Charlium, Ho Charli-ol-e-um,
Divorce and contra-cep-ti-um.

And NOW they're thunderin' to the finish—
And it might have been a photium
Except for P-R votium, Ho Charlium.
RED Robbin piped the Leader
And she took home the troph-i-um,
What a catastroph-i-um for Ho Charlium.

AND SO the moral of this tale is
DON'T COUNT UN-HATCHED EGG-I-UMS,
T'll/you have it in the bagg-i-um, Ho Charlium.
FOR instead of having chickens—
You'll have yoke upon your facei-um
And end up in disgrace-i-um, Ho Charli-i-um.

CHORUS
Ho Charlium, Ho Charli-ol-e-um,
Divorce and contra-cep-ti-um.

YET de Valera's dream came true,
In spite of Brian Len-i-hum
And all of Charlie's, men-i-um, Ho Charlium;
FOR, got his comely maiden dancing—
But she's up in Áras an Úachtar-um,
And the athlete at the crossroads[81] was Ho Charl-i-um,
The athlete at the crossroads is Ho Charlium.

Ho Charlium, Ho Char-li-o-le-um,
We got our comely maiden dancing—
But she's up in Áras an Úachtarum,
And the athlete at the crossroads was Ho Charlium,
The athlete at the crossroads was Ho Charlium.

CHORUS
Ho Charlium, Ho Charli-ol-e-um,
Divorce and contra-cep-ti-um.

© *Fintan Vallely*

Between 1812 and 1818, the then British Secretary for Ireland Robert Peel set up the first police force, in Ireland of course—The Royal Irish Constabulary, from which the Northern Ireland RUC derived its name. The natives in their day commemorated Peel's name by calling the cops "Peelers"[82], a term which spread to London with the setting up of his police there in 1829, and which survives to this very day in Belfast. It seems that the already-mentioned Darby Ryan *(Shades of Ashgrove)* was arrested and jailed after being out on a banned demo against the Tithes Act of 1830. Furious at the insult to his learning and dignity, on his release Ryan swore revenge, and lay in wait in the long grass. Eventually along came a puck goat out gallivanting "on the *seachran*'[83]. The noble beast was wrestled to the ground and impounded by a Bansha Peeler patrol for some reason or other, and Darby got wind of the story. The rest is history. By the following Sunday he had *The Peeler and the Goat* written, printed and distributed. It was a *White Christmas* success, and was being trilled on every lip in the locality. All the political discontent of the times was invested in the song and Darby became a hero. His first concert performance of the number was done standing on the back of a horse, and his words were rapidly disseminated throughout the length and breadth of the land, being amended here and there to give local flavour. The song appeared too in exile in America and even Australia, much to the disgust of the authorities who bate the shite out of anybody they found singing it. Many were prosecuted, and eventually the song's sentiment towards the Peelers was compressed to what was described as "a humbugging sort of a smile which outraged the dignity of the law". This too was considered potent enough to be illegal, but the ballad singers did well out of the affair even if they suffered a bit. *The Melbourne Argus* eventually offered a reward for the authentic version of the song, and like the USA's '78 records which validated many's the fiddle and flute player, so was 'The Peeler and The Goat' given the imprimatur by agencies abroad. The father of the source of these notes, Jeremiah Grogan of Bansha, a grandson of the Bard, verified all of this for that newspaper to give the reader here now the opportunity to learn the skit anew. The song has been updated to take in goats' current suffering at the hands of the traditional music industry, which in search of their hides has them as terrorised as rhinoceroses. The Angora cardigan industry too is hunting the female of the species—to enforce conception by implanting fertilised Angora eggs in the rugged wild nanny wombs. All profits from this song will be donated to the 'save the goat' campaign supported by asthmatics, bodhrán haters, sean-nós singers, pipers and smart-alecks nation-wide.

***

The Peeler and the Goat

The Bansha peeler went out one night on duty and patrolling-O
He spied a goat upon the road who seemed to be a strolling-O,
With bayonet fixed he sallied forth and seized him by the wizen-O,
Swearing out a mighty oath he'd send him off to prison-O.

"Oh, mercy! Sir," the goat replied, "Pray let me tell my story-O,
I am no rogue or Ribbon man, no croppy, Whig, or Tory-O.
I'm guilty not of any crime, ne'er petty nor high-Treason-O,
And I'm sorely wantin' at this time, for 'tis the rantin' season-O."

"It is in vain you do complain, or give your tongue such bridle-O,
You're absent from you're dwelling place—disorderly and idle-O.
Your hoary locks will not avail, nor your sublime oration-O,
For Grattan's Act will transport you by your own information-O."

"O, the Penal Laws I've ne'er transgressed by deed or combination-O,
I have no fixed place of abode, nor certain habitation-O.
Bansha is my dwelling place where I was bred and born-O,
Descinded from an honest race, therefore your threats I scorn-O."

"I'll soon chastise your impudence and insolent behaviour-O,
Well-bound to Cashel you'll be sent where you will find no favour-O.
Impartial Billy Purefroy will sign your condemnation-O,
And from there to Cork you will be sent for speedy transportation-O."

"This parish and this neighbourhood are peaceful, quiet and tranquil-O,
There's no disturbance here thank God and long may it continue so.
Your oath I don't regard a pin to sign my committal-O,
For my jury will be gintlemin and grant me an acquittal-O."

"Let the consequence be joy or woe, a Peeler's power I'll let you know,
I'll fetter you at all events, and march you off to prison-O.
You villain sure you can't deny before a judge and jury-O,
That I on you found two long spears which threatened to in-jure me-O."

"I'm certain if you weren't drunk, on whiskey, rum or brandy-O,
You would not have such gallant spunk, or be so bould and many-O.
You readily would let me pass, if I'd the sterling handy-O
To treat you to a poteen glass—O it's then I'd be the dandy-O."

"Well, that was back before the bodhrán then when "TORY" meant
    subversion-O,
And our goats feared neither jig nor reel and set-danced for diversion-O.
But now the drunken peeler's been replaced with worse coercion-O,
Bombastic, batterin bullies with Ó Ríada's foul percussion-O."

By Darby Ryan; Last verse © Fintan Vallely

The well-worn story of 'The Ould Orange Flute' tells of how a flute could only play the one kind of music, the Orange anthems upon which it had been weaned. Crawford Howard here updates the concept to the age of recording technology and consumed music, to at least the 1960s when the electric motor was the source of all melodic power (an mp3 version is expected by 2020; it will deal with how The Ould Orange Mac refused to be PC enough to download from i-Tunes, on account of the "i"), The antithesis of the Peace Process, the concept is that old dogs cannot be taught new tricks.

***

The Fenian Record Player

Wee Willie John MacFaidin was a loyal Orange lad,
He thought that Ian Paisley was the nearest thing to God.
He thought they ate their childer in the backwoods of Ardoyne,
And he knew that history started with the Battle of the Boyne.

One night he took a brick in his hand and he wandered up the Falls
Whistlin' *Up the Rangers*, and singin' *Derry's Walls*.
He bust a big shop windy to annoy the Pope of Rome
And he took a record player and then he staggered home.

Next night they held a hooley in the local Orange Hall
And Willie took his player to make music for the ball;
He chose a stack of records of a very loyal kind
But when the music started up he nearly lost his mind.

For the Fenian record player was a rebel to the core;
It played the tunes an Orange all had never heard before:
For *Derry's Walls* and *Dolly's Brae* it didn't care a fig,
It speeded up *God Save the Queen* till it sounded like a jig.

It played the *Boys of Wexford* and *The Wearin' of the Green*.
Such turmoil in an Orange hall had never yet been seen.
It played the *Woods of Upton* and *The Men of '98*
But when it played *The Soldier's Song* it sealed Wee Willie's fate.

223

For the boys went clean demented, to the ground wee Will was thrown,
And they kicked his ribs in one by one to the tune of *Garryowen*.
They threw him out the windy to *A Song of Ould Sinn Féin*
And they kicked him all down Sandy Row to *A Nation Once Again*.

But the rebel record player was heard no never more
For the loyal lads left in there knocked it to the floor,
But yet it was not finished, and the funniest thing you've seen—
The flashes flyin' out of it was orange, white and green.

Wee Willie's up in Purdysburn, he's crazy as a coot,
He's sittin' there in his padded cell and tootles on his flute;
And when he goes to play his flute he always gets it wrong,
For halfway through he always finds he's playin' *The Soldiers Song*.

There's a moral to the story, what it is I cannot say;
It may be just the ancient one that 'crime will never pay'.
If you ask Wee Will MacFaidin, he says, "Ah, crime be blowed!
—If you want to pinch a record player, do it on the Shankhill Road!"

© *Crawford Howard*

The Arab Orange Lodge

(Air: 'Wearin' of the Green')

Oh, a loyal band of Orangemen from Ulster's lovely land
Could not march upon the Twelfth, processions was all banned,
So they flew off to the Middle East this dreadful law to dodge
And they founded in Jerusalem the Arab Orange Lodge.

Now Big Ali Ba who charmed the snakes was the first recruit,
John Names McKeague from Portglenone learned him to to play the flute.
And as the oul' Pied Piper was once follyed by the rats
There follyed Ali till the Lodge ten snakes in bowler hats.

Now they made a martial picture as they marched along the shore,
It stirred their blood when Ali played 'The Fez Me Father Wore';
Then Youssef Ben Mohammed hit the Lambeg such a bash
It scared the livin' daylights from a camel in a sash.

Well, the movement spread both near and far, there was lodges by the score,
The Jerusalem Purple Heroes was the first of many more;
The loyal sons of Jeddah and the Mecca Purple Star,
The Risin' Sons of Jericho who never touched the jar.

Now the banners too was wonderful though' some would make you smile:
King Billy on his camel—as he splashed across the Nile;
But the Tyre and Sidon Temperance had the best one of them all,
For it had a lovely picture of Damascus Orange hall.

The Apprentice Boys of Amman marched beneath the Blazing Sun,
The Royal Black Preceptory was jet-black every one,
An' lodges came from Egypt from the Abu Simbel Falls,
They shouted, "No surrender! We'll guard old Cairo's walls."

But when the ban was lifted and the lodges marched at last
The Arabs were decided for to march right through Belfast;
It caused a lot of trouble before they got afloat
They could not get the camels on the bloody Heysham boat.

Camels choked up Liverpool, camels blocked Stranraer,
And the Shiek of Kuwait came along in his mile-long motor car.
But the Eastern Majic LOL, they worked a crafty move;
They got on their magic carpets and flew into Aldergrove.

When they came to Castle Junction where once stood the wee kiosk,
They bought up Royal Avenue to build themselves a mosque;
Devlin says to Gerry Fitt, "I think we'd better go;
There's half a million camels comin' down from Sandy Row."

Now the speeches at the field that day was really somethin' new,
For half of them were Arabic and half was in Hebrew,
But just as colonel Nasser had got up to sing The Queen,
I woke up in me bed at home and found it was a dream.

© *Crawford Howard*

Wee White Turban

(Air: 'The Broad Black Brimmer')

'Twas a bundle that was hangin' in what's known as 'Father's tent',
A bundle of striped material black and red,
And when I asked me mother now just what it did contain:
"It's your father's Bedouin uniform," she said.
One day she made me try it on, (a wish of mine for years)
"In memory of the ould boy, son," she said,
And as I put the kaftan on, she was smilin' through her veil
As she wrapped the wee white turban round me head.

CHORUS:
It's just a wee white turban he wrapped around his head,
Forty yards of good material there and more,
An old Kaftan that he stole in Marrakech,
A pair of boots he used against the Camel Corps,
An old curved sword in its sheath of camel hide,
A wavy dagger he used against the foe,
When it comes to blood and gutters, the man that really matters
Wears the wee white turban of the PLO.

'Twas the turban that me father wore in the desert long ago
When he left me mother's harem on the run,
'Twas the turban that he wore when he stood by Nasser's side
When he put the British Army on the run.
The Brits were sendin' aeroplanes and SAS men by the score,
The Suez Canal belonged to them, they said.
But your da swam to the tanker, lit the gelignite and sank her,
And claimed the canal for Egypt then instead.
CHORUS

It was two miles from Damascus when he made the final stand
Surrounded by his enemies ten to one.
As he lay in the sun there bakin', he knew there'd be no prisoners taken,
And the ammo for the AK nearly done.

A Joe Walsh Tour from Knock Airport did arrive,
Comin' in to re-fuel goin' slow.
Your da hijacked the Boein(g), "To West Belfast," he says "we're goin,'
Flyin' the wee white turban of the PLO."
CHORUS

© Joe Mulheron

No TV soap can ever hope to compete with a good news story, and no news story is as good as a local cops and Provos one. Evelyn Glenholmes hit the headlines in April of 1986. A (British) *Sunday Times* article had claimed that she was a wanted woman in England. Eventually an extradition warrant arrived in Dublin requesting the pleasure of her company in London. However it was seen by the court to be invalid, so the judge ordered her release. Meanwhile Douglas Hurd expressed his intense concern that Ms Glenholmes should come on over anyway, and assured the Gardaí that a proper invitation was on the way. The Guards decided to keep in touch, so about five thousand of them crowded around her like wasps on jam as she, legally, left the court. Some journalists and political associates joined in too, and the whole tumbling schemuzzle careered off through Dublin, gathering numbers and momentum with every new street it entered. Radio covered it with live comment and update news flashes. It ended up in British Home Stores, of all places, where customers ran screaming for their lives as Special Branch men with guns dug in in the Lingerie Department. Finally an undercover 'branchman' cracked, and blasted off into the air. No one, least of all the Gardaí, knew who he was—the uniformed cops dived for cover thinking he was a Provo, the Sinn Féiners thought he was SAS. He ordered everyone to lie on the ground, and Fergal Keane, a press correspondent, who asked him for an interview got only a two-word reply and a third shot fired past his ear hole. Finally the convulsions subsided and he was led away babbling later to have his then-impending promotion honoured by transferral to organising car-parking in the Garda HQ or something. The new warrant finally arrived, but it too was invalid. "Bang-Bang" was a Dublin 'head' who, until the late 70s, used to go along the street whipping out an imaginary pistol at intervals shouting "Bang, Bang!"

***

Bang Bang's Day

(Air: 'The Wee Drummer')

The papers inform us of what's goin' on
In Cape Town, Managua, Belfast, and Saigon—and
They tell their own versions of truth, lies and facts—but
Once headlines are printed there's no goin' back.

It all started one day in our 'National' Press
(God save th'English *Times,* and her editor bless—for
Exposin' mad women in Ireland at large
While Margaret in London needs people to charge.

"You're nicked, at long last," *The Mail* said with glee;
"Till you're an ould woman, no green fields you'll see.
For when TV and newspaper hype is all done—
You're bound for the mainland on ex-tra-dish-ion."

CHORUS:
Oh, I'm the wee man in the white coat[84] you saw
Cullin' the seagulls[85] for *Érin Go Bráth.*
Ye Patriot shoppers[86], lie down on the floors,
I'm Bang-Bang, the guardian of British Home Stores.

But bad luck befell us that awful Spring day,
For the judge in the court case let her get away.
One ould ignorant gulpin[87] that just for the thrill
Dared question th'integrity of the Ould Bill.
CHORUS

So we rang up Douglas, and to him "Fair play!"
He got us new warrants, the very next day—but
Pat MacIntee[88] twisted the law then once more;
"Let her go!" says the judge, and he walks out the door.

The laws had run out, we could not get our way,
So we locked her in court[89], kept her friends all at bay,
But we were backstabbed by that beak once again, for
He smuggled her out the side door to the lane.
CHORUS

Her crowd gathered round and the hunt then began—
She was led along by Ireland's 'most wanted' man,[90]
While the TV and Press charged along by her side, askin
"If you escape, can you say where you'll hide?"

Round the Four Courts in a car then she sped
Driven by joy-riders—mad in the head.
We ordered all traffic to block that crowd in, but
Those cars were determined to help Glenholmes win.
CHORUS

At last, with great tact, we put her off the road.
She took to her feet with a great crowd in tow,
Runnin' round Parnell Square makin' one awful din—till
In Sackville Street we had them all hemmed in.

Now it was bad enough image to have tearin' around
A crowd of Irregulars[91] 'bout Dublin town,
But when on Prince's Street she turned into a door,
My mouth fell open wide—it was British Home Stores.
CHORUS

I gasped out in horror; how could she so shame
The pomp and the glory of that famous name?
Oh! What would Rupert Murdoch and BBC say?
"Guards let BHS Shop Fall to IRA."

There was nothin' else for it—so I pulled out me piece,
For Anglo accords all this madness I'd cease;
As I squeezed on the trigger, blood rushed to my head;
By Christ! What a feeling! My day it was made!
 CHORUS

I let off two shots, Boys oh Boys! What a scene—
Shoppers and coppers all started to scream.
While I grinned to meself: "Jesus, this is the stuff!"
The Guards all surrendered, Glenholmes had enough.

I let off another one just for the crack,
But none of the Press had the nerve to shoot back.
When my ambulance came, I'd all under control,
And now I'm promoted to callin' the roll.
CHORUS

© Fintan Vallely

Mahon's Mice Are At It Again

(Air: 'The Mice Are At It Again')

People of Ireland hear my tale, it's your ex-Taoiseach in St. Luke's,
I'm in a spot for memory lapses got to do with books.
Like an organ grinders' monk-ey Mahon can't be shook,
They have no grasp of business, dealing, chance or fluke.
I told them—
The mice are at it again, as sure as notes are notes,
They were at it in Charlie's land and shirts, his dinners, ties and coats.
They drove poor Lawlor to the 'Joy, we were all the time complain -ing,
But there was no getting away for the mice were at it again.

Since the Irish top cat's gone with mice we're over-run,
Tho' we've set up traps and tribunals, poison pens, but still no-one
Can stop the scratching, leaks and squeaks or hunting that's been done
To find out where stray cash goes to or where it's coming from.
For the mice are at it again, as sure as cash is cash,
They're in and out of the safes and drawers through the pockets in the wash.
I tried to throw some light on things, but it was all in vain,
For as soon as I told a story, Oh the mice got at it again.

For administrative convenience didn't they chaw up Charlie's cheques,
And in the nineties chawed my nearly fifty grand of debts.
They chawed an eight grand sterling gift and fifty under the bed,
And bewildered all the punters, and the Dáil, so I said:
"The mice are at it then, as sure as gifts are gifts,
Digging out and digging in, depositing for thrift.
They have my daughters persecuted and Cecelia wrongly blamed,
All chawed down to nothin', Oh the mice are at it again.

And now they have my memory chawed up, I remember less.
Teflon tablets are the only man to cure the stress.
But the punters still support me and believe I've made no gain,
So I face the traps in Mahon's as a civilian with no shame, though

The mice are at it again, as sure as out is out,
They've chawed me down from Taoiseach to back bencher in a rout.
Reputation chawed to pieces now, my good work all in vain,
Oh say a prayer for Bertie, for the mice are at it again.

© *Fintan Vallely*

Part 20: Advertisement

"And so in conclusion
It may seem amusing
This subject confusing to now fantasise..."[92]

and include Eoghan Ruadh O'Súilleabháin's advert for the sale of a horse. Author of florid ballad-stanzas denouncing the Penal Laws and other tyrranies of his day, this flamboyant, prolific versifier led a colourful life and died at the age of thirty-six in June 1784.

Saturday, the sixteenth of September, Seventeen Sixty nine, will be sold or set up for sale, at Skibbereen, the stalwart stallion Spanker, the property of Thomas O'Donnell Esquire. Strong, staunch, steady, sound, stout, sinewy, safe, serviceable, strapping, supple, swift, smart, sightly, sprightly, spirited, sturdy, shining, sure-footed, sleek, smooth, spunky, well-skinned, sized and shaped sorrel steed of superlative symmetry, styled 'Spanker', snip square-sided, slender-shouldered, smart-sighted, with a small star, and steps singularly stately; free from strain, sprain, spasms, string-halt, stranguary, sciatica, staggers, scaling, sollander, surfeit, seams, scouring, strangle, strenuous swelling, soreness, scratches, splint, squint, squirt, scruff, scales, scurp, scars, scabs, scarred sores, scattering, shuffling, shambling gait or symptoms of sickness of sordid sorts. He is neither stiff-mouthed, shabby-coated, sinew-shrunk, spur-galled nor saddle-backed, shell-toothed, slim-gutted, surbated, skin-scabbed, short-winded, splay-footed or shoulder-slipped and is sound in the sword-point, and stiffle-joint, has neither sick-spleen, sleeping-evil, set-fast or snaggle-tooth, nor suppression of urine, sand-creaks, swelling-sheath, subcutaneous sore, or shattered hooves, is not sour, sulky, slow, surly, stubborn, or sullen in temper, neither shy, sly, skittish, slow, sluggish, nor stupid. He never slips, stripes, strays, stalks, starts, stops, shakes, swells, snivels, snibbles, snuffles, smarts, stumbles or stocks in his stall or stable, and scarcely or seldom sweats, has a showy, skittish switch tail or stern, and a safe set of shoes to stride on. He can feed on stubbles, sheaf-oats, straw, sedges and Scotch-grass, carries sixteen stones on his stroke with surprising speed over a six-foot sod or stone wall. His sire was the sly, sober Sydus, on a sister of Spindle Shanks by Sampson and Sporter, son of Sparker, who stole the Sweepstake and Subscription Plate last season at Sligo. His selling price is sixty-six pounds sixteen shillings and sixpence sterling.

Sincerely supplied (subject to suitable situating), by Ó Súilleabháin-disciple Éamonn Ó Bróithe.

APPENDIX

The Binder Twine Song

(Schitheredee version)

There's one great invention, it is my intention
In song now to mention so listen a while;
It has so much potential, I'd say it's essential
To carry it always whatever your style.
For farming 'twas made but 'twill suit any trade,
It comes in three colours and simple design;
You just cut it to size as each new need arise-es,
And the greatest surprise is—it's just binder twine.

Now it may be amusing to find me enthusing,
This subject perusing in verse and in rhyme,
But I think it a scandal the wheel and the candle
Had no song to praise them since they were designed.
You have read of computers of high specif'cation,
There's thousands of books on Professor Einstein,
But since it now seems his wife wrote those complex equations;
I'd rather be praising th'oul binder twine.

For twine's other dimension is trouser suspension
Or stretched out in tension by farmers as gaps,
But what's worth more than a pension is Begley's intention
Like Christo with twine the great Blasket to wrap.
For tying in a hound or for squaring out ground,
For banjo and fiddle strings gone in decline,
Such versatile uses are surely exclusive
To that profusive extrusion they call binder twine.

Now, excuse my transgression for I've been digressin'
And I've a confession and it is no lie;
Last year on the road between home and Listowel
My fan-belt gave out and white steam hit the sky.
Stop-gap engineerin' suggests to repair them—
A good pair of tights should just do the job fine.
Ah, but I didn't have mine on this sad occasion
So I strung it up with some ould binder twine.

You've heard of the builders of Egypt's great Pyramids,
How they wrought for ages on those steep inclines,
How those boulders they'd hustle and jostle with muscle
And push and adjust them till they were in line.
'Twas the slaves done the labour all tethered together,
With the weight of those iron chains they must've been cryin';
Wouldn't they have worked faster if only their masters
Had not been such bastards—and tied them with light twine.

And so in conclusion I find it amusing
This subject confusing to now fantasise,
In dream and conjecture about our electors
Who voted in members who ply them with lies.
We should be concerned surplus twine isn't burned
For from it could be made a gallows so fine;
Then we'd gather together those birds of a feather
Their throttles to tether with stout binder twine.

© *Mícheál Marrinan, Tim Lyons, Fintan Vallely*

The Night-Clubbing Song

(Schitheredee version)

I sing of the capers of rockers and shapers
Who're out all the night 'till the break of the day;
Some just out of the cradle, and more hardly able,
In every night-club they are boogeying away
They're screeching and arguein', jostlin', blaggardin',
And some in these places are quite indiscreet;
Where the lights are all flashin' the music is crashin'
In this latest fashion of imported beat.

These clubs I'm relatin' will sure take some batin'
With no band atall but D J and machines:
He's n'er pipes nor melodeon, but sits on a podium,
Guitar, drum and keyboard gush out on the scene.
And it's not surprisin' when the music starts risin'
To see him put mufflers on each of his ears,
While those that are dancing and maybe romancin'
Are losing their hearing forever I fear.

Now, if you must aks me or maybe attacks me
For finding myself in such iniquity,
Well, my wife went away with mates from th' ICA
To do knitting and sewing and plan a Guest Tea.
So I hopped into my suit and away with me foot-
To-the-board, in the Escort I hit Dublin heat;
After map-read in wrangles, I found a star-spangled
Night Club called 'Bojangles' in Low'r Leeson Street.

Underground in that cellar were lassies and fellas
Knockin' back bottles and bawlin' for more,
The price was ferocious, too high to get stocious,
So I tried precocious-ness on the dance-floor.
But at three in the mornin' without any warnin',
As under the glass ball I tasted new life,
There, with a Georgio Armani-clad sleazy
Majorca-tanned geezer was my darlin' wife.

238

In due recognition she winked in a fashion,
For the eyelid on my side was all that was free.
There was no chance us talkin' with that music squawkin',
'Twas just as well then that we'd both have a spree.
But the shapes we were makin', if I'm not mistaken,
Left our legs achin' for half the next year
Jivin' and boppin, with leppin' and hoppin',
No trace of a set-dance to cheer up the ear.

I love to be dancing the Polkas, the Lancers,
In Kerry the slides, in Clare hornpipes and reels,
And what's seldom seen now—like a horse with a plough—
What I wouldn't give for a few double-wheels.
So I'm grateful for those who're explaining and training
Revived old-style dancing with informal poise;
No-more I'll be complaining of boredom and dreaming
Of gaming in night-clubs with young girls and boys.

© Michael Marrinan, variations Fintan Vallely

Willie Mac Bride You Bastard You

(Schitheredee version)

Oh, youse know that big long song about Willie MacBride,
Well, to tell yis the god's truth, it turns me inside,
You'll hear it on the Shankhill, you'll hear't on the Falls,
And mostly from people who can't sing at all,
You go out to the pub on a Saturday night,
For a pint and the crack, a-and things are all right
'Till some boy with his shirt out
Slumps down by your side —and says:
"Zing-zzz z'wunn zbouzz Wllee Mmm-Bride,"

Ah, you say you don't know it (but this will not do)
For his plan all along has been to sing it to you.
He knocks over your drink, and takes off in a key
That wasn't constructed for Pava-Rotti;
And with the lines grinding on, Oh, the horror gets worse,
As it slowly sinks in—that he knows every verse.
With his arm round your shoulder, by now he's your friend—and
He's determined to sing this damn thing to the end.

CHORUS:
Did he sing the song badly?
Did they gulp their pints madly?
Did we all fall asleep before we'd finished our round?
Did the barstaff cry, "Last drinks" to stir us?
Did the punters cry, "Thank God it's o-o-o-ver"?

You slip out to the jacks for a quart'r of an hour,
Kill time at the TV set out in the Bar,
And then you sneak back thinking he might have tired,
But he's still choking on gas, tangled up in barbed wire;
And for ten minutes more he continues this rant
Again, and again, and again till you can't
Care that he's up to his oxters in gutters in trench—es, or give
Two tupp'ny damns where the red poppies dance.
CHORUS

240

Oh, Willie MacBride why the hell did you die?
The trouble you'd have saved if you'd come back alive.
If you'd got a good job, or signed on the b'roo—
We wouldn't have to endure this ould mush about you.
Aye but maybe it's better for you that you're dead
With the green fields of France piled up over your head;
For the trouble you've caused us since that day you died,
Oh, rusty shrapnel's too good for you, Willie MacBride.
CHORUS

And you—Eric Bogle, just what was your game?
White crosses mark out the road to your fame.
Could you not guess the Fureys might drive us insane?
Can you not call them off?—Jasus, we're not to blame!
And why d'you complain about shellfire and smoke?
Sure with PA and cig'rettes, the pubs are no joke.
Where we drink to his mem'ry each weekend we're broke
Makin' Willie Mac Bride's fans consumptive ould soaks.
CHORUS

© Crawford Howard, variations Fintan Vallely

Songs And Summaries

THE ARAB ORANGE LODGE (p. 225)—Crawford Howard's fantasy concerning the consequences of exporting the L.O.L. to Damascus.

THE BALDY SONG (p. 145)—On the plight and restorative antics of men who can't handle baldness.

THE BALLAD OF BINDER TWINE (p. 24)—Micheál Marrinan's verbal extrusions on what to do with the EC Twine mountain.

THE BALLAD OF RANGY RIBS (p. 27)—Dungiven bard Brian McGuinness's exhaustive dissertation on the colourful life of an unkempt, unbiddable, unwanted bullock.

THE BALLAD OF THE TEETH (p. 147)—Tale of how he lost them to the desires of a jackdaw, and then got them back.

BANG BANG'S DAY (p. 229)—Blow by blow saga of the exciting scenes surrounding Evelyn Glenholmes's release from court in the late 80s Dublin.

BEAUTY SPOT GLANLEA (p. 179)—Patsy Cronin's imaginary journey around the world, based on reading newspapers and atlases.

THE BODHRÁN SONG (p. 54)—Tim Lyon's tale of the fate of a German tourist who went trying to make his own bodhrán.

BOOTLEGGING BOGLE (p. 22)—Sheila Miller lashes out at the folk-pop song pirates of folk club Scotland.

THE BUFFALO FARM IN ACHILTIEBUIE (p. 114)—Andy Mitchell's nightmare about Scottish Highlands development after overhearing a pub discussion on EC grant-aid for bison farming.

CHARLES THE NAVIGATOR (p. 199)—Charlie Haughey's conquest of the Mizzen head by yacht.

THE CITY OF MULLINGAR (p. 186)—A 19th century hedgeschool master style eulogy on that most gorgeous of Irish cities.

CONFESSIONS OF A BODHRÁN PLAYER (p. 52)—Observations on the contradictions and absurdities with which the vegetarian bodhrán player must grapple.

THE DAFFODIL MAN FROM KILTYBANE (p. 136)—Jim McAllister's effusions on an innocent who happened to suggest something so *effete* as flowers to a Crossmaglen publican.

HO CHARLIUM (p. 213)—The course of the 1990 Presidential election seen as a horse race at the Phoenix Park.

INVITATION TO A FUNERAL (p. 45)—The Finnegan's wake theme—the corpse doesn't turn up, but the crack is good, and rows and fights reduce the party to patheticism.

THE IRISH JUBILEE (p. 106)—A post-famine food-hallucination of over-eating set in Irish America.

THE JOHNNIES SONG (p. 64)—How the Gardai set about shutting down the dreaded Well Woman She-been.

LAST NIGHT'S FUN (p. 20)—A repertoire of 102 tune names all set to the tune 'Phil the Fluter's Ball'.

LEITRIM IS A VERY FUNNY PLACE (p. 162)—How the natives of Ballinamore dared to refuse to talk to RTÉ in the heat of crisis.

MAHON'S MICE ARE AT IT AGAIN (p. 232)—Bertie Ahern blames mice for the mystery of the missing money.

THE MAN FROM DEL MONTE (p. 166)—Scorching cynicism from the sadistic quill of master-bard Déaglán Tallon.

THE MICE AT IT AGAIN (p. 39)—Sean Corcoran's collected woes about the proliferation of mice in the days before Dak and poison.

MICK SULLIVAN'S CLOCK (p. 150)—The Clock packs it in, goes on tour and is beaten to death.

THE MILTOWN COCKROACH (p. 34)—Con Ó Drisceoil's fate at the fangs and venoms of beasts of the night in a tent.

THE MISSING MISSUS MYSTERY (p. 131)—How Mrs. Runcie never appeared on the TV when the Bishop went to Rome for the early stages of an Anglico-Roman cease-fire agreement.

THE MOVING STATUES MOVEMENT (p. 129)—The only economic growth of the 1980s—when even the statues got sick of the rain.

NELL FLAHERTY'S DRAKE (p. 71)—Spectacular curses over the theft of a prized bird.

THE NIGHT THEY RAIDED OWENY'S (p. 77)—Finbar Boyle's satire on the Gardaí for daring to close down a famed topers' emporium in Dundalk.

THE NIGHT-CLUBBING SONG (p. 94)—Mícheál Marrinan's jaunt to the big smoke to taste a bit of the high-life and late-drinking fashionable in 80s Dublin.

Notes

1. Georges Denis Zimmerman puts this poetically on p. 113 of his *Songs of Irish Rebellion:* "Broadside ballads may have the life of a soldier crab passing from one shell to the other". Thomas Davis, quoted in M.J. Barry's *Songs of Ireland,* wrote of the business of matching tune and words: "In all cases the tune must suggest, and will suggest to the lyricist, the sentiment of the words ... The sound of the air will always show the current of thought, its pauses and changes". With political song, the air—if the song is popular—becomes associated with the political sentiment, and acquires a life independent of its music qualities: it becomes a 'party' tune, and no words are needed to evoke the sentiment of the original text. One such is 'The Peeler and the Goat'.

2. *The Sunday Show,* RTÉ radio, Easter Sunday 1991.

3. *The Era,* quoted in Peter Bailey's *Leisure and class in Victorian England* (Toronto, 1978), p.165.

4. This is a catalogue of The Gintry begun in 1826 and still continuing. It's purpose is to give status to self-importance within the Anglo and Anglo-Irish, less-than-Royalty caste in society. This helps them weed out the weaklings in courtship so they can maintain their (divinely-ordained) snobbery, genetic patterning and ill-gotten wealth within their ranks. The plain people nowadays however are fighting back with 'Genealogy' and the like. This is basically a way of doing the same thing, only it actually generates money (mostly American dollars) where it had never been before. Effectively it is a tax on faraway, third- and fourth- generation emigrants for being just that. These people, whose homes are in America or Canada, nosey around every summer and put the shits up the hard-working namesakes back on the ould sod, making them live in dread that somebody they don't know is going to claim a cup of tea, a day's eating, the house, or maybe even the farm. Both this and Burke's should be properly and accurately described as 'the sperm trail'—since it is only male surnames that are being followed, thus leading into the type of delusion which had Ronnie Reagan declaring that he was descended from Brian Boru.

5. "We have to break this 'Ulster Style' of singing ... it's not singing at all. It should be kept to the back rooms of pubs"—adjudicator.

6. The Ordnance Survey share this location (the Phoenix Park in Dublin) with the other great institutions of Irish life—the President, the Vatican, the Gardaí, the American Ambassador—and the Zoo.

7. Phillip Luckombe, *A Tour Through Ireland...,* London, 1783, p19; quoted in *White Britain and Black Ireland* by Richard Lebow, Institute for the Study of Human Issues, Philadelphia, 1976, p 41.

8. James Page, *Ireland: its Evils Traced to their Source* (London, 1836), Vol.1, 10, quoted in Lebow p42.

9. Henrietta G. Chatterton, *Rambles in the South of Ireland*, London 1839, Vol. 1, p10, quoted in Lebow, p42.

10. *The Times*, 13/10/1846, quoted in Lebow p 48.

11. *Fraser's Magazine*, March 1847, 373, quoted in Lebow, p40. But modern research shows that there is Celtic blood in the English, and that the Irish may not be Celtic at all, only carriers of Celtic culture.

12. *Thoughts on Ireland* (London, 1847), 6, quoted in Lebow p59.

13. *Punch* magazine, XIV (1849), 54; XVII (1851), 26, 231; quoted in Lebow p40.

14. Henry Inglis, quoted in Lebow, p43.

15. From John Carr's *The Stranger in Ireland. A Tour in the Southern and Western Parts of That Country in the Year 1805*, PA 1806. Quoted in Lebow, p 45 (this Lebow is some boy).

16. Yosser, the wayward, hyper and impulsive hero of Alan Bleasdale's *Boys from the Blackstuff*, notoriously, in perpetual search for work, would say "I can do that". And of course he could—after a fashion.

17. Tourists who have not the local language always seem to think you've asked them where they've been. Their reply is simply an international 'default' answer, for they know well that there's a 99% chance that that's the question you did ask them.

18. Shoes.

19. A commercial device which does with chemicals and without hair what Mary Magdalen did for Jesus.

20. Commercial plastic explosive.

21. Flute player Kenny Hadden from Aberdeen is reported as arriving late into a concert at a point when a piano accordion player was accompanying a lad playing the saw. He is alleged to have been overheard whispering in a loud voice to an accomplice who had held a seat for him: "Ah! My favourite combination, a piano accordion—and a saw."

22. The equivalent of calling a piano "a Pie? Ah, no!" This is a popular incorrect pronunciation, a fine demonstration of pure ignorance.

23. Superstitions.

24. An Irish version of a hobgoblin. Related to Puck, the mischievous sprite or demon who is related to an image of the devil, after which a Puck (Billy) goat is named, and for which association one is captured and stuck on top of a pole at Puck Fair in Killorglin, Co. Kerry, every August while people revel all around.

25. African drummers.

26. In the quaint language found in Ireland, somehow impossible to teach despite the proliferation of French, German and Spanish, this word means "song".

27. Transcription and music from *Lillibulero* Vol. 2, Ulster Society, 1988, p30.

28. The referendum' is a process peculiar to Republics whereby those who want

a change in the law have the opportunity to take part in an intelligent debate to alter people's minds, the whole thing being then put to a vote. Counter-demonstrations therefore, with the object of stifling information dispersal, are not in such a situation intended to be part of the process.

29. The former minimum height for entry to the law enforcement profession.
30. Militant International anti-abortion body.
31. They sell everything from baby food to shrouds, butter to axle grease, Bisto to rat poison, lemonade to peroxide.
32. A lavatory cleaner which kills everything in shight, and, we are told, out of sight too.
33. In 1988, licences to import 8 million condoms were applied for.
34. Half of the workplaces set up in Ireland since 1987 employing more than 100 people are non-Union.
35. Storyteller John Campbell provides the Encyclopaedia (Mullabanica) definition of 'Gulpin': "I was doing the MC at a concert in Mullaghbane one time and I had been out at the hay all day till late. I was starving and had just the time to jump into the suit and away. I got through blethering about the first couple of acts, and in the middle of the second I noticed somebody bringing a big plate of boiled ribs down below to the dressing room for one of the visiting performers. After my spiel the next time I lifted back the tea towel just to have a peep at the food, and before I knew it—all the ribs were gone. I had hardly finished sucking the last one when I heard the guest coming down the ladder. So I hopped into the wardrobe and didn't your man come over to the tray, pull off the cover. 'CAMPBELL! The fuckin' gulpin!' is what I heard him say."
36. In December 1993, John Taylor, Official Unionist M.P. for Strangford, Co. Down, in excruciating attempts to define northern protestant identity, declared that a compulsive condition he described as "jigging at cross-roads" was a prime distinguishing characteristic of Irish ethnic identity.
37. Ancient Irish mythic folk warriors. They used to belong to the IRA, but now the UDA have said that they were really protestants, loyal to the British Queen, and actually constructed the border themselves to keep the wild southerners out.
38. Jews harp
39. Scottish Highlands and Island Development Board, the guilty conscience of the descendants of the people who cleared all the original Highlands inhabitants out to Cape Breton, Nova Scotia where they are now fomenting cultural revolution and a whole new mythology that will eventually occupy the minds of all mainland Scottish musicians.
40. In Autumn 1995, the Church of Ireland acknowledged the existence of such over-zealousness by an apology to the people of Ireland. But in fact many men of Irish surnames had already changed religion in order to get their hands on the family seat in an earlier era.

41. An indulgence is a period of remission from a place called purgatory where, if you have committed 'venial' (wee) sins, you go for a while as a kind of embarkation lounge before heaven (after you die, of course)... There the temperature s only 250—300 degrees F (Gas mark 1—2), as opposed to Hell where it is 425—450 (Gas mark 7—8).

42. There was one apparitive incident in the North of Ireland—in Ardboe, Co. Tyrone in 1955; it was seen by two protestants, so it must have been the real thing.

43. The Met office reported the worst rainfall in history, in 1879 , on 125 out of 183 days between March and September.

44. A dance Mecca in the West which never did have a dance on a Friday. Sabotaged by licentiousness, turntable spinners with sunglasses and drug-culture, its robust Irishness is now long gone. These days it caters for people who want to get depressed 'out' by providing ballroom dance in a drink-free environment.

45. The original air to this song—'Football Crazy'—was written by James Curran who was born in Moville, Co. Donegal in the first half of the 19th century. At the age of four, anticipating the Great Famine, and emigration which was to produce tear-jerkers like 'Glenswilly' and the TB ravages which created 'Noreen Bawn', he took the boat for Glasgow where he became a prolific Musichall songwriter. Having completed hundreds of songs he decided to take to the stage himself, but died soon afterwards when he realised the kind of people he had been writing for. Most people believe that the song is from the 1960s, but in fact soccer was a big game in Glasgow in the 1800s. And it still is. Andy Mitchell tells the story about the comedian who normally 'did' the Rangers social club on a Saturday night, being invited to play in Celtic's—as a special effort to 'bring the communities together'. He was aware on the grapevine that on the night before his show someone had broken into the Celtic club and robbed the big screen and the VHS machine. On coming in the front door he was welcomed by the committee and found himself stuck for conversation. But never short of a quip he pointed to the life-size figure of a bloody Jesus crucified on the cross (which in the Rangers' popular imagination hangs in the Celtic club) and remarked, "I see ye got the bastard that nicked the video..." Celtic won the Scottish FA Cup in 1989, and Margaret Thatcher happened to be presenting the trophy. The Celtic fans were wildly chanting "Maggie, Maggie, Maggie, go to fuck..." The Radio Clyde commentator politely reported, "The fans are ecstatic. They're chanting 'Maggie, Maggie, Maggie, best of luck ... or something which rhymes with that.'"

46. The Catholic Church's attitude to divorce, abortion and the Angelus (the holy picture with campanile accompaniment which precedes the evening news on RTÉ television) was, until late 1995, also the law of the land in Ireland. Those who were less than happy with this situation weren't all in the DUP.

47. In 1981, allegedly on behalf of the Bulgarian Umbrella Manufacturers' Association, a Turkish man Mehmet Ali Agca tried to shoot the Pope in St. Peter's Square, Rome. Some time later John Paul visited him in jail to let him know what he *really* thought of him.

49. 'Dealing'.

50. A play on the mad dog disease and 'Reavy'. Ed Reavy was a Philadelphia-Cavan tunesmith whose music is famous.

51. The Credit Union is a strange institution which on the one hand encourages people to save, and then turns around and gives them money out on loan.

52. The most campaigned-for man in Irish history. Now at the zenith of his powers he became a councillor in Arklow where the conservative parties were so jealous of his topping the poll they wanted to recruit him.

53. A kind of gun that looks like a 'big-bale' tractor prong.

54. On the TV programme the local postmistress/telephonist was shown as having great humanitarian concern for political prisoners held in the Maze Prison.

55. A famous horse that was held to ransom the previous year. Money was paid for him to a Garda in a swindle, the money disappeared and it is rumoured that Shergar was served up as hamburgers at the next year's Willie Clancy Week.

56. Prince August Moulds. Often presumed to be a brewery or cheese factory, this business makes solid pewter models to cater for the market of people who never want to grow up. The Orange Order's GHQ in Belfast in 1992 had hundreds of such wee soldiers in its public area. These were in a glass case, disposed over a large-scale sculpted and landscaped Diamond area (Co. Armagh) battle-terrain.

57. All information from a wonderful booklet produced by one of his descendants, Sean Ó Grúagáin.

58. A total mess.

59. I am indebted to Bríd McSweeney of Cill na Martra for this information. She also relates the story of the time that friends had come in to clear the house for the 'Station'—a tradition in which the ungrateful clergy, having had the faithful squander all their savings for centuries on building chapels, then turn round and insist that mass has to be said in their houses as well. The two fiddles were put out in the barn with other stuff. At the end, seeing as there was a crowd assembled they thought they may as well have a bit of a dance, but on going out to get the instruments didn't they find that Patsy's was broken. "It broke its sides laughing at yours!" he said to the brother.

60. A West Cork version of a Jacobite song. If the country ever gets rid of the 'Soldier's Song' anthem (odious to the rugby-playing class, and for which its writer Peadar Kearney had his patriotism rewarded in royalties) it stands a good chance of being the Nation's next tonal representation. While it has the advantage that, being traditional, no royalties would have to be paid, it has

the disadvantage that Charlie Haughey supporter Donie Cassidy ambushed it and committed it to the slavery of a Fianna Fáil election jingle ('Arise and Follow Charlie', which people kept on doing up until 1997) a ditty that is so banal it is impossible to forget. In any case, now that half of England has been forced to listen to 'Amhrán na bhFiann'— and Linfield supporters too—thereby subliminally learning it, because of the World Cup and soccer, the State may well decide to hang on it, especially since they now own the copyright.

61. Part of the earliest hurriedly-introduced safety procedure.

62. 'Duty-Free'.

63. During storms, for some reason, the loos on ferries always seem to get clogged, so forcing you to roll up your trousers. The loo rooms are themselves like shallow tanks to avoid spillage out onto the other public areas.

64. Ideally you throw up into the sea rather than into the airlines' sophisticated, paper bag technology.

65. Cheap airfares were begun mercifully by Ryanair and continued by Richard Branson (who also brought us condoms too).

66. Traditional emigration was forever and there would be a wake. But at least you got rid of the bastards—nowadays they keep arriving back for 'holidays' five times a year, splashing around money, keeping the rest of us up half the night with their whinging and yapping, distracting us from our work and causing us to feel like inadequate paupers.

67. After singing this song in McCarthy's of Baltimore one night some years later, this singer was approached by the jovial lifeboat man-of-the-moment who described the good-natured shipwreck victims on that day as "all looking the same—typically ashen-faced and unremarkable", but when offered a customary cuplet of brandy, Charles J. guffawed, identified himself and displayed for his benefactor a bottle of Hennessy taken off the wreck in his duffel bag.

68. The lighthouse keeper who helped the survivors survive their good spirits and summoned the lifeboat was made redundant after, and had to emigrate.

69. The 'taypot' is the one he gave to dear Margaret Thatcher (thereby leaving an embarrassing gap in a set in the National Museum) but she told him to get stuffed anyway. The 'talks and lunch' refer to the same cratur.

70. Marine Vessel.

71. Market Research Bureau of Ireland—they do straw polls to test how the gullible public are responding to PR blitzes, lies and slander regurgitated by the media.

72. Sir Charles' own radio-interview description of the impact with the Mizzen. These matters suggested the following letter to the editor of *The Miltown Journal* (07, 2000) from a Cork wag:

Dear Sir,

May I, through the medium of your esteemed organ, appeal to the genius responsible for 'Dunne's Story' and 'Charles the Navigator' to tie the two great men together in a new magnum opus. You need not be short of a title—"Ben There, Dunne That, Shopped the Taoiseach", although not original, would do nicely.

Yours etc, A Herring.

73. Ronnie had been in Ireland before once when still only a filmstar.

74. Enterprising local entrepreneurs came up with the brilliant idea of selling little plastic bags of local muck to the visitors. Some foolish tourists, who ate the stuff thinking it was cup-a-soup, had diarrhoea for weeks and ended up feeling like authentic famine victims.

75. A Ballyporeen publican is in on the act with a pub called after him. It is inundated with so-called cynics every year who are afterwards compelled to brag, each sentence of course carefully opening with a denunciation "I was in that fuckin' kip, and you know what..."

76. 'Bandit country' in South Armagh, where idle people had nothing to do but sit around looking at vast, purposeless, flag-flying, military installations and eventually, out of over-familiarity and boredom, figure out a way to destroy them, whereupon the authorities built bigger and better ones ... and so it went on until the Peace Process turned the lot into Art installations.

77. An expensive clinic in America, the Mayo Clinic; there Brian had a liver transplant. As a 90-year-old interviewee of RTÉ's Donncha O'Dualaing said: "That man should be home in his bed—not runnin' around with another man's liver in him."

78. A famed English Grand National jump. A supporter of Brian at the time was quoted as saying of his lapse of memory: "All Brian Lenehan's slip was worth was three Hail Marys and an act of contrition."

79. Hal Al Meats, a Co. Mayo specialist Islamic meat factory he was involved in establishing.

80 "The Lord is on our side—I feel it in my bones ... it's going to be 'Winner alright!'—Brian Lenehan, Sunday after-mass meeting, 4/11/90; reported RTÉ *News at One*.

81. The 'crossroads' and 'comely maiden' references are the images from the corrupted version of the vision of Eamon De Valera, one-time president, only dragged in because Robinson parodied one of them in her victory speeches.

82. The term 'peeler', funnily enough, is also a 16th century expression for a thief—'to strip of possessions'.

83. On the raz, seeking a nanny (goat).

84. He was dressed in a Louis Copeland white casual jacket, subtly contrasting dark trousers, Dunne's Stores tie, and socks by Penney's. His accessories

included a Smith and Wesson revolver, laminated identity card, chromed hand cuffs and a matching set of Granada car keys.

85. He missed everybody.
86. Initially there was controversy at British Home Stores opening a branch in Dublin on account of the 'British' bit. So they compromised and changed their name to BHS. They eventually left anyway.
87. In these circumstance the word also means 'ignoramus'.
88. The defence barrister.
89. Gardaí blocked her exit from the court.
90. Kevin Mallon, another tabloids' Provo fantasy-figure.
91. The Pro-Treaty (Partition of Ireland, 1921) word for the anti-Treaty IRA, which was used by the old guard of Fine Gael until their demise.
92. Tim Lyon's amendment to Mícheál Marrinan's wonderful binder twine ballad.

Fermanagh singer Rosie Stewart entertaining her father Packy McKeaney with 'Invitation to a Funeral', at the Derrygonnelly Singers' Weekend in October, 2000.

Photograph © Fintan Vallely

Founded in 1985, the Dedalus Press is one of Ireland's longest established and best known literary imprints, dedicated to new Irish poetry and to poetry from around the world in English translation.

The publication of *Sing Up!* is both a new departure for the press and a recognition of the many and diverse ways in which the lyric impulse finds expression in the Irish psyche.

For further information on this and other Dedalus Press titles,
as well as a selection of poems and songs for free download, please visit
www.dedaluspress.com.